Supreme Deception

Sybil Fletcher Lash

An original publication of Sentinel Productions

Sentinel Productions
P. O. Box 1509
Lawrenceville, GA 30046-1509

For information, address:
Sentinel Productions
P. O. Box 1509
Lawrenceville
GA 30046-1509

ISBN: 0-9718831-0-6

Cover art & book typeset by:
Image of God Publications (770)365-8754

Printed in the United States of America.

Contents

Acknowledgments

I would like to thank some of the people who helped make this book a reality. Georgia Right to Life for directing my efforts when it came to unearthing the facts. Also my deepest gratitude goes to the National Memorial for the Unborn for supplying the arguments before the court both December 13, 1971 and October 11, 1972.

To my husband, Bryan, who supported this entire effort, both emotionally and financially. He is the most honest person that I've ever met and his encouragement has carried me through.

To my daughters for their continued efforts to help keep this story alive, and for the joy they bring me in being a part of their lives.

Thanks to Dr. D. James Kennedy and Father Frank Pravone for their encouragement and leadership in the Pro-Life cause.

To P. R. Bailey for his help early on in helping me organize my thoughts and sharing his writing skills with me.

Finally to my dear friend and prayer warrior, Pam Glanton, whose continued heart felt prayers had a large part in the spiritual guidance I received.

Foreword

I want to tell you about a very special friend of mine. Her name is Sybil Lash, and this book tells about the two of us and the work that we do together.

I am Mary Doe, the woman who was used to legalize late term abortion. I have been trying to get people to listen to me since 1973 when the *Roe v. Wade* and *Doe v. Bolton* decisions were handed down. *Doe V. Bolton* made abortion possible through all nine months of pregnancy.

In 1996 God sent Sybil and Bryan, her husband, into my life. They are, I believe, God's gift to me. They have researched my story and proved that I never sought an abortion, I never had an abortion, I have always believed abortion is wrong. It is murder.

Sybil is my best friend and my guardian angel. She helps organize me when we speak. She travels with me. I trust her as I have trusted no other friend. Because of her I've seen the world through different eyes. She and Bryan believed me and are standing with me. I have help and hope now. The truth will be known and this deception will be revealed and made right.

You will learn in this book how I was used by a lawyer to legalize a procedure that was never my wish or desire.
Sandra Cano

Introduction

In these pages you will learn how a poor, uneducated, vulnerable woman was used by our judicial system to legalize the murder of the innocent. Her name is Sandra Cano, her court case name is Mary Doe of, *Doe v. Bolton*. Her case was the companion case to Roe v. Wade. They were heard the same day before the U. S. Supreme court.

Both legalized abortion but Sandra's case legalized late term abortion.

When I first met Sandra and heard her story I had great difficulty believing anyone could be treated so unfairly by an attorney. I heard her tell me her story on more than one occasion and her facts never changed. She stated over and over again that she never believed in abortion, never sought an abortion and never had an abortion. My husband Bryan and I decided we could prove her story true or false if we had enough facts. We merely believed her enough to dig for the truth. The deeper we dug the more legitimate her version of events.

Sandra has been tenacious in her efforts but it has cost her family and friends. It has put her safety in peril. She has been threatened; her personal property vandalized, and even under gunfire while she held her grandchild in her arms. I have asked myself many times if I could be as steadfast and not given up after so many years.

We are friends. I travel with her and help organize her thoughts when we speak. I don't think for her and I don't put words in her mouth. She would never allow anyone to alter this injustice that was done to her. What you will learn in this book are the facts of Sandra's circumstances and how they were misrepresented before the highest court in our country.

I would ask that you read this book no matter what your position on abortion. Once you have the information, please think what she has been through. Judge for yourself if you think she received justice. Would you want this kind of justice if you were in her shoes? None of us can comprehend what it must be like to carry the burden of guilt she carries or the deep frustration she experienced of not being believed.

Bryan and I promised Sandra that we would help get her story out. Once you are finished reading this book you will know the truth behind the *Doe v. Bolton* case. In the appendix you will find the oral arguments of her case before the U. S. Supreme Court. Read for yourself how another version of the truth was presented before the justices. Sandra is not the only woman that bears the results of this case. You will learn the truth of what all these women carry. Their fears, their shame, and how they were manipulated at the hands of the abortion providers. Just like Sandra, they too, were told half- truths and were deceived into make a life long decision with few or no facts. They too fall prey to <u>Supreme Deception</u>.

1
Early Departure

It's dark, just before 5:00 A. M. I turn off the alarm before it has an opportunity to send its shrill sound into the early morning stillness. Every time Sandra and I make another trip, I awaken every hour on the hour with the anxiety I feel over making the flight or not getting to the right place at the right time.

Sandra and I are going to tell her story again. It's about abortion. It's about lies and being used. It means telling the personal pain of Sandra's life. But babies are dying and women are still victims. So I feel my way through the dark house. I have left Sandra's phone number downstairs again

Sandra Cano has become a good friend and someone that I deeply admire. She is the real "Mary Doe" of *Doe v. Bolton*, the companion case to *Roe. Wade*, the two United States Supreme Court decisions that legalized abortion. Both decisions were announced the same day, yet most Americans don't even know about *Doe v. Bolton*.

Sandra's life is dedicated to telling the truth about the lies and deceptions involved in the *Doe v. Bolton* case, even though she supposedly "won". Her fight means Sandra must guard her privacy, living in fear for her family's safety. No phone book contains her name. Only those she trusts know her address. She was once shot at while holding her grandchild on her front porch. She has had her car vandalized because of her stand. She shuns the spotlight and lives in an underground type existence.

But today she will make one more dreaded airline trip to tell a story she is convinced must be told. And as usual, she has asked for my help. That's why I stumble my way to my kitchen at 5 A.M. to call her.

Sandra's case changed the face of United States law. While *Roe v. Wade* left the states some authority to prohibit abortion in the last three months of pregnancy, *Doe v. Bolton* effectively removed that authority by its broad definition of 'health'. Partial birth abortions are based on *Doe v. Bolton*. Yet Sandra never wanted an abortion. All she wanted was legal help to get a divorce and regain custody of her two oldest children. Sandra was used and misled. She was misrepresented before the highest court in the United States. Why did this happen? Sandra believes her lawyer wanted someone to fit her own plans. Now all Sandra wants to do is set the record straight.

Many have asked, "Who is the woman named on this case? Is she a strong feminist? Is she driven to achieve abortion rights? Has she become rich and famous? I've heard these questions and others like them so many times, and the answer is simply

"No." Sandra is an uncomplicated person. She doesn't enjoy notoriety. She wishes that she could avoid the controversy her story stirs up. All she wants to do is get her story out, right the wrong her case has caused, and then go home and continue to raise her "special needs" grandsons.

Sandra's case helped divide this nation into two camps: "pro-life," or those against abortion; and "pro-choice," those wanting abortion to be legal. While many abortion supporters claim they only want to spare women from the burden of an unwanted pregnancy, it is a fact that eliminating the unborn has proven to be a very profitable endeavor. On the other side of this chasm rests close to forty million children in the U. S. alone who were never given the right to life. And there are so many women who underwent abortions and now struggle with feeling they were pressured and used at the most vulnerable time in their lives. These women suffer emotionally and physically, yet they have no protection or recourse under the law regarding the misinformation, physical pain, emotional suffering and botched procedures that have left many ill and even sterile, because of *Roe v. Wade* and *Doe v. Bolton*.

Sandra suffers. She knows all too well that these procedures are allowed because of a court case that supposedly represented her. But the case was a lie. Sandra never wanted an abortion. She was used because she was too poor, too desperate to do anything but trust her lawyer. So now Sandra fights the only way she knows how, by opening the private areas of her life over and over again as she speaks to groups willing to consider the truth about her case.

I go downstairs without turning on a light, shuffling sleepily through our house, feeling my way into the dark kitchen. The dull light over the stove blinds me as I dial. He answers. I never know how much of what I say he understands because he only speaks Spanish. The only word he says is "Sandra". She is given the phone. She is already awake. She always is before one of our trips. I assure Sandra that I'll pick her up in an hour. Then I paddle off quietly to shower, dress and pack.

The dogs have taken my spot on the bed and are all settled in. "Bear," our Golden Retriever, has her head on my pillow and little Auggie is on his back with all four feet in the air sound asleep next to my husband. Bryan understands that I have to help her. When I first told him of Sandra's plight he looked at me across the kitchen table and simply said "Alright Sybie, we'll help her." He has been totally supportive of our commitment to Sandra. He never questions a trip and is my greatest source of encouragement when I get frustrated or discouraged by the lack of action on Sandra's behalf.

2
Sharing Her Story

As the shower drags me awake, I recall the first time Sandra told me her story. She has been trying to get the world to listen to that same story for over a quarter of a century. When she first told me her story, she was nervous about the old concerns: of not being believed, being considered stupid that such events could go on without her knowledge. Because of these concerns, the facts came out in a random order. At the first meeting she brought a friend who just sat there silently, but Sandra felt more confident with this woman in the room.

The second time I heard the story was a few weeks later, Sandra again just talked and again there was no time line. The events of her life were related running from the past to present and back again. When I sat down with my notes there was one overwhelming constant, the facts never changed. No matter how disturbed the time line, the facts remained the same. She has written judges and telephoned anyone she thought might remotely help her. I admire her tenacity. While I dry off and dress, I can't help but wonder if other people would continue on and not give up in the face of what Sandra has encountered. I finish packing, slip from the house, get in my car and drive into the early morning fog.

The eldest of six children, Sandra grew up poor in Atlanta. Her early life began to build the desperation that caused her to become the vulnerable centerpiece in *Doe V. Bolton*. Because of financial problems, Sandra's family lived with grandparents who suffered numerous infirmities. Sandra's mother was some times overcome by the stress of the family's circumstances. Being the eldest child, Sandra sometimes became the focus of that frustration and stress. Her mother's experience of being overwhelmed by her circumstances and her difficulty in coming to grips with that frustration set a pattern for Sandra's life. Throughout those early years, Sandra's attempts to alleviate her Mother's suffering filled her childhood.

School proved unbearable for Sandra. She was poor, over-weight and suffered from Bell's palsy, a condition that often left half her face paralyzed and drooping. To avoid the ridicule she faced each day, Sandra finally dropped out of school in the ninth grade. Her mother tried to force Sandra to return to school, once even breaking a broom handle across her daughter's back as the two argued in the front yard as the bus arrived. But Sandra's formal education had ended.

Within the next few years Sandra married the first man she ever kissed. On their third date, Joel asked Sandra to go meet his grandmother. Sandra's parents thought she was traveling a distance of fifteen miles from Atlanta. Instead they received their daughter's call when she arrived in Oklahoma many hours later. Outraged, they ordered Sandra home with the threat of having Joel arrested. When the pair quickly returned, Sandra's parents first beat her with a belt, then drove the couple to Centry, Alabama, for a quick marriage ceremony. It was a matter of family honor.

A week later Sandra found out Joel was on probation for child molestation. Although she tried to make the marriage work, her husband continued in and out of jail under different child molestation charges throughout their six years together. Joel was never dependable in providing for his wife and the children she eventually bore him. Because of his criminal behavior, Sandra never felt safe leaving her children alone with their own father. Then when her first child was only a few months old, Sandra's father died unexpectedly. To Sandra's disbelief, her mother remarried only three weeks later to a stepfather who made it quite clear he did not want Sandra and her family in his life. She was devastated in a way I can barely grasp. The only security she had ever known was gone.

How did it feel to be that vulnerable? I think about those days as I drive down Interstate 85.

3
Getting The Records

The car is always a safe haven on a cold morning. It carries me to her modest home. I'm a little uneasy in this part of town and am always grateful when Sandra's new husband walks her to the car. He makes her feel a little more secure and a little less alone as he carries her suitcase out of the house.

Sandra will miss the comfort of her routine and the two "special needs" grandchildren she is raising. She has promised to bring them a gift. Preparations for a trip are so involved for her. She has to stock everything they will need during her absence because her husband doesn't drive and the children make our leaving emotionally stressful for Sandra.

We are quiet as the car travels on. I'm not sure what Sandra is thinking. As for me, I think about the role I play in Sandra's life.

I am not Sandra's manager. I am her friend. I help when she travels and assist her as she shares the truth about her involvement in the abortion controversy. Sandra and I came together from totally different directions. My life's work, after being wife and mother, developed as a public advocate for the causes my family and I believe in so deeply. I am an activist. Sandra is a victim. Our strong friendship has taken us much farther. Now when Sandra goes out to speak I travel with her and help her present her story in a way that keeps the details chronologically correct and the focus on the main points she wants to communicate. But I have to smile at any suggestion I could ever put words in Sandra's mouth. She will not allow anyone to distort or change the facts she works so hard to tell. I may help Sandra speak, but no one speaks for Sandra.

Sandra's audiences include widely diverse groups such as legal workers, political activists and church congregations, often combined together. For many years following the 1973 *Doe v. Bolton* decision, Sandra was ignored because she only had her word to dispute her lawyer's side of the story. Then in 1988, Sandra got her court records unsealed. She went to the courthouse where they were kept and asked the clerk how to go about finding out about her case. Only then did Sandra finally know how she was used and deceived when she was most vulnerable.

For a short time afterward Sandra was the focus of various media. She was interviewed in newspapers and on television. She traveled to other states to tell her story. Surely, she thought, if people knew the truth about her case they could help get this legal misrepresentation resolved. In the end, nothing changed, except that Sandra began to suffer as the threats and, later, the violence against her began.

It constantly amazes me that the popularity of an issue seems to depend more on such things as good marketing and "political correctness" rather than facts. If Sandra's situation had happened to someone with money or prestige, the wrong would have been righted over a quarter century ago. But at that time Sandra was naive, ignorant and vulnerable, with neither the resources nor the outright ability to get the truth out.

4
How She Is Seen

We arrive at the airport ninety minutes ahead of flight time. We've learned the hard way that we need the extra time. I surprise Sandra with a new pair of comfortable shoes, a gift from a friend. It would be out of the question for Sandra to spend enough on herself for a new pair of shoes. She is raising two grandsons who have special needs and her husband is a day laborer. The shoes fit well. She is grateful for them. Without the welcome gift on her feet she would be walking the long way to the gate in pain, but without complaint. Eventually, I'd know by her limp that she was in pain. That is just the way she is.

Once we were late for a flight and the only parking spot I could find was quite a distance from the terminal. As we scurried along, dragging our small suitcases behind us, we spotted an abandoned wheelchair. Sitting Sandra in it, I piled both suitcases in her lap and pushed as fast as I could. One wheel rubbed against Sandra's leg, and she finally asked me to slow down. We laughed and laughed at the sight we must have presented. We made the flight but learned we must allot more time. Lessons learned.

Today, as usual, people stare at Sandra as we hurry through the airport. She is heavy and I watch as some passing people turn on her with stares, whispered comments, half-hidden laughs and looks of disgust. I hope Sandra doesn't notice. Travel is difficult enough for her. She doesn't need to be made to feel anymore uncomfortable than she already is. Sandra refuses to respond to the looks, except to apologize to me. "Oh, Lord," she gasps as she gets very winded at our pace and becomes flushed. "I must embarrass you."

Reaching our gate we show our drivers licenses for identification. This is the only reason Sandra travels under her own name. Otherwise she fears pro-choice activists will find her again. She refused to stop speaking out when her car was vandalized with painted graffiti and, when she faced threats and name-calling. It was only after she was shot at with her grandson in her arms that she realized the danger.

Once we are seated at the gate Sandra begins to look for the pilot to arrive and board the plane. She prefers the older ones; the more experienced the better. If a younger pilot boards our plane she'll look at me nervously. She also looks to see if the pilots appear well rested. I'm not sure how this is all judged, but I know from her countenance how her judgment goes.

It's too bad the judges in Sandra's case didn't apply the same scrutiny to the evidence and facts presented in her court hearings. Things could have turned out differently, and we probably wouldn't be sitting in this airport, waiting for our boarding call to begin.

Our seat numbers are called and we make the slow walk down the ramp to the plane's forward door. We try to stay to one side as business travelers pass us as they adhere to their busy schedules. To them air travel is a part of everyday life. To us it is an endeavor packed with challenges.

Our assigned seats are halfway down the plane. As we enter, we quietly request a seat extension for Sandra. The regular seat belts are just too uncomfortable for her. As we make our way down the aisle, I watch the faces of some passengers as they see us coming, the eyes that plead, "Please don't sit in my row", and the look of total relief as we pass on by them. Sandra and I usually joke about their reactions. Sandra never judges them and is always relieved when our seating doesn't interfere with another passenger's space.

We finally arrive at our row, where we have the window and middle seats. Sandra likes the window to make it easier to sleep but she never requests it. Only after I have insisted that I have no preference does she choose her seat. After the flight attendant goes over the safety features Sandra is handed the demonstrator seat belt for her seat extension. The plane finally rolls along the runway, and after all the rush we begin to relax. We have made the flight.

Speaking will be difficult for Sandra this time, and I'm glad as she nods off for a short nap. She has been battling bronchitis for the last few days and has not slept well these past nights. She hates traveling, between being away from the grandchildren and the stress of telling her story, she's exhausted. On top of her illness she has thoughts that she will sound and looks like a hillbilly. This only means that today's trip is an especially uncomfortable one for her.

And then Sandra worries about her husband. He just doesn't understand her intensity about this issue. He wants her to stay home and be with the children. He resents being sole caretaker while she is away. He also becomes jealous and worries out loud that these trips may lead to her finding some other man. She and I share our disbelief at such an idea. Hurting someone else is the last possible thing on Sandra's mind. Besides, our time is always so limited on these trips even for the people we are supposed to meet. All we ever seem to do is run from one place to the next, from the car to the airport gate, to the plane, to the hotel, to the meeting, back to the hotel, to the airport to the plane back home.

Sandra would never purposely break a promise, yet alone a marriage vow, without justification. Sandra never accepts any speaking fees, only reimbursement for travel expenses. The only income her family has is from a small disability check and her husband's day labor wages, but a recent injury has kept him from working. Sandra's life of financial difficulty continues today.

But money is not her motivation. Sandra's worst fear is that she would hurt anyone. Though she hates to leave her family, even for short times, she does it, because she knows so many women have been hurt because of her court case. Sandra was used to make abortions legal by being misrepresented before the highest court in America.

The plane levels off and the little drink cart makes its appearance. As the flight attendant works her way down the aisle dispensing drinks and pretzels, Sandra is staring at her. The flight attendant notices and Sandra is concerned that the woman will wonder why. The flight attendant gets to our row and Sandra wants the woman to know that her airplane earrings are what captured Sandra's attention. In that moment I know that Sandra notices the stares she receives and that those stares hurt. But she would never want anyone else hurt in that way, so she explains to the flight attendant why the stare. It would be a much better world, if what we are as a person on the inside, mattered more than how we look on the outside. It would be a much nobler goal to fine-tune one's character instead of one's waistline.

We get our drinks and open our worn file folder to review what we'll address at the upcoming meeting. She'll be tired this time, making the time line of events blur in her presentation. That's where I come in, as her friend and helper. After a brief introduction Sandra and I will step to the podium. I'll ask her questions, which she will answer. This is Sandra's favorite format. Her audience will get to see Sandra's personality as well as hear her story, and hopefully they will come away admiring her as much as I do.

5

The Affidavit

Even after all our time together, I am still amazed that in the American judicial system a case like Sandra's can get as far as the U. S. Supreme Court without the plaintiff being properly represented or identified. For the thousandth time I ask myself how the Supreme Court can decide a case where facts are misrepresented or not presented at all, how an individual's circumstances could be used to change standing law when that change had nothing to do with what the plaintiff originally sought.

When Sandra became pregnant with her third child, she knew clearly that she could not depend on her first husband or her family for support, financially or emotionally. Wanting her child to have a better life, she made the heart-wrenching decision to give up her child for adoption. When she became pregnant with her fourth child, her stepfather announced he had endured enough. He then gave inaccurate information to authorities to have Sandra's two oldest children placed in foster care. Sandra was frantic and desperate.

She went to Atlanta Legal Aid asking for help. She wanted to obtain a divorce from her child-molesting husband and to regain custody of her children from foster care. There she was introduced to Margie Pitts Hames, an attorney who led Sandra to believe she would work hard to achieve her divorce and regain her children. Little did Sandra know that Pitts Hames was planning a major woman's issue case, an attempt to legalize abortion.

Sandra believes Pitts Hames was looking for someone desperate enough not to ask questions, someone who probably wouldn't understand the technical legal jargon her paperwork would involve. She planned to hide her true intentions by promoting the excuse she needed to keep her plaintiff's identity a secret.

Sandra was so relieved to finally have some capable authority figure say she would help her. She trusted her attorney and signed every paper Pitts Hames put in front of her without question. She approved anything to help speed her case, get her divorce and regain her children. To Sandra's surprise, her mother began working with the attorney, and as her family began to accept her once again Sandra grew even more trusting. She believed she would win her divorce and get her babies back soon. When someone is desperate enough, they are vulnerable to people who promise a solution to their problems, individuals who portray themselves as powerful trustworthy figures. I can't help but wonder how many others have been used as Sandra was.

Sandra insists that no one, at any time, went over the contents of the attorney's papers with her. Records show she never once testified in court. She remains amazed that no official of any court ever asked her face-to-face what the case was about. If they had, she would not have carried this burden for over a quarter of a century.

During one conversation with Pitts Hames, Sandra was surprised when she was briefly asked about her stand on abortion. Sandra was confused on why such a question would come up in a case about divorce and child custody. Sandra gave what she thought was a reasonable answer that would pass over what she saw as an unrelated topic. Sandra said that she did not believe in abortion for herself, but she couldn't say for anyone else. To Sandra's relief, the matter was apparently passed over. In fact, Sandra's sister has stated that at that particular time Sandra didn't even know what an abortion actually was.

Today, Sandra believes that the lawyer was trying to get her to volunteer words that could be used to benefit the arguments for abortion.

In the legal hearings that followed Sandra appeared in a courtroom only one time, as part of a group of pregnant women who remained seated and silent. She was never identified or singled out in any way. In fact, the only evidence filed in the case that supposedly came from Sandra was an affidavit signed May 5, 1970. That affidavit will be addressed during Sandra's presentation when she speaks tonight. This is how that affidavit describes Sandra:

"I am presently pregnant with my fourth child and am very disturbed at the thought of carrying another child, as I feel I cannot care for the child properly. I am very nervous and upset at the thought of raising another baby. I cannot cope with the responsibility of caring for another child. It drives me almost crazy to think about it."

"I have two children in a foster home because I was unable to care for them. I adopted out a third child last year. I feel I cannot love another baby and I am depressed all the time thinking about my pregnancy. I do not want another baby."

"I have been a patient at Central State Hospital in Milledgeville (Georgia) and I am afraid I will end up there again because I am so nervous over being pregnant. My health is poor and the thought of carrying another child for nine months and having to give it up again makes me feel like crying all the time. I know if I had to give another baby away I would end up in Milledgeville for sure. I understand an abortion is a dangerous thing and that there are risks involved in performing an abortion, even under the best of circumstances. Knowing all these risks and problems, I still desire an abortion."

"I feel that after this abortion is performed that I do not want any more children. I desire to be sterilized, in any manner the Doctor sees fit, at the same time as the abortion is performed.

Sandra refutes this affidavit point-for-point in nine specific parts.

(1) Sandra was not "nervous and upset at the thought of raising another baby." That statement is simply a lie. Sandra was nervous and upset at having to live with a convicted child molester. She was nervous and upset about not knowing how her babies in foster care were doing or who was watching them. She even worried about simple things like whether or not the foster caregiver remembered how her children liked to be put to bed. The affidavit begins with a lie and simply continues.

(2) The affidavit states that she "cannot cope with the responsibility of caring for another child. It drives me almost crazy to think about it." As Sandra says, this is an out-and-out lie. Sandra always asks me to consider why she sought out a lawyer to get her children out of foster care and returned to her if she could not cope with the responsibility of caring for her own children. When the time came to place her next children up for adoption, she didn't go crazy. She made a difficult decision based on what she believed was best for her children.

(3) The affidavit continues by stating "I have two children in a foster home because I was unable to care for them." The only reason Sandra's children were in foster care was due to information furnished to authorities by Sandra's stepfather, who had made it well known he did

not want either Sandra or her children around. The affidavit gives the impression that Sandra willingly put her children in foster care, which is compounding the lie.

(4) The same statement stresses that Sandra "was unable to care for" her children. Again, this is simply not true. These words have hurt Sandra the most. At the time her children were taken from her Sandra was gainfully employed. She has never been on drugs or abused alcohol. She has always tried to be the best example she could be to her children, regardless of the circumstances. Her life has been one long sacrifice for others.

(5) Another affidavit statement says, "I have been a patient in Central State Hospital in Milledgeville." This is factually true but very misleading. Central State is a mental hospital. Sandra was there for a few days to be observed. She has never been readmitted. The misinformation given to the hospital, which led to Sandra's observation, came from her stepfather, the same person who had her children placed in foster care.

(6) The affidavit supposedly quotes Sandra as saying "I know if I had to give another baby away I would end up in Milledgeville for sure." Sandra did place this baby for adoption. It was heart wrenching and difficult but Sandra wanted to do what was best for her child. And for the record she did not wind up in a mental institution.

(7) The affidavit states that "I know an abortion is a danger-

ous thing and that there are risks involved in performing an abortion, even under the best of circumstances." It is an absolute lie to say Sandra knew such things at that time. Sandra was never told about the effects of an abortion at any time throughout the legal process, yet alone that her case was about abortion. In fact it seems ironic that such a statement was ever included in the argument for abortion, since the mental and physical risks of abortion are not told to women. They are not even told of the medical or physiological risk; e.g. breast cancer or post abortion syndrome. Special laws have had to be passed so that a woman can know the identity of the abortionist

(8) The affidavit continues, "I desire to be sterilized." Again, the affidavit includes a lie. Sandra's attorney and her mother forced this decision, and it did happen. Sandra found herself alone in a hospital room after giving birth to her fourth child whom was given up for adoption. Her husband was not around, being in trouble with the law again. At this most vulnerable time she was again pressured by people who wanted to control her life and use her circumstances for their own gain and was sterilized.

(9) Finally, the affidavit highlights the statement, "Knowing all these risks and problems, I still desire an abortion." This is the height of all the lies contained in the affidavit. Sandra's lawyers did try to arrange an abortion for her before the case was heard in an Atlanta federal court.

Horrified at such a plan, Sandra fled to her husband's family in Oklahoma to avoid being forced to have an abortion. She only returned to the Atlanta area once she received assurances that she would not have to undergo an abortion.

Lies, and more lies! And Sandra pays the price of those lies each and every day.

Sandra never had an abortion. On November 7, 1970, Sandra gave birth to a baby girl and gave her up for adoption. As for Joel, he remained in trouble with the law as he kidnapped and molested children three times in six weeks towards the end of 1970. Joel was apprehended and pleaded guilty on January 21, 1971, he was sent to prison and subsequently served 10 years.

On May 17, 1971, Sandra's divorce was granted. She had been married six years and the union produced four children. Joel died in November of 1988 at the age of 46.

6
Lack Of Facts

Our plane arrives and our host is waiting for us. We check into our hotel room and Sandra immediately heads for a long, hot, uninterrupted bath. I know of no one who enjoys this little ritual more than Sandra does, for this brief time she will be alone with no demands on her.

While she enjoys her private time, I think back to when I first read the transcript of the case's arguments presented before the U.S. Supreme Court. How can it be possible that someone wanting a divorce and the rescue of her children from foster care could be so misrepresented by a lawyer? Was the deception so easy that all that was needed was an affidavit included in a stack of papers Sandra signed in simple trust?

In oral arguments before the Supreme Court, Dorothy T. Beasley, representing the State of Georgia, made several statements that leap out from the transcript to even a non-lawyer like myself. They include:

"We know of no facts. There are no facts in this case. No established facts."

"It is not a complete divulgence of the facts surrounding her (plaintiff's) circumstances."

"We know of no facts about her at all."

And finally, "No interrogatories were answered, no proof was submitted."

Twice the justices asked if "Mary Doe" was a real person. Pitts Hames, responded, **"Yes your honor,"** and referred to the affidavit that Sandra points out was so full of lies. Dorothy T. Beasley, arguing on behalf of the baby, was asked the same question and her response was **"I don't know, we know no facts."**

And yet in spite of these statements, the court continued with the case.

7
Pressure On Politicans

The only parallel that I can personally draw on is from my experience in the political arena. I have witnessed some politicians ignoring facts when it comes to legislation. Allow me to explain.

In my background I have some appreciation and understanding of the pressure put on those in the political arena. I have lobbied for five years and I served as a legislative aide for six years in my home state of Georgia. I was an aide to Representative Kaye of the 37th House district. I got to watch closely how laws are introduced, debated and either passed or rejected. I was very fortunate to work for an intelligent and honest man.

Representative Kaye always wanted facts to back up every opinion. He would listen to opposing views but in the end relied on the facts and the desires of his constituents to make a final decision. There are others I have encountered who are unwavering in their stand to defend and protect the Constitution of the United States. I do think that we need more men and women to run for political office who will carry out the intention of the Constitution to secure freedom and rights for the Sandras of this world: the vulnerable in our society.

They must be unyielding in their stand because great pressure is put upon them. Individuals and groups enter this arena with the sole objective of furthering their own causes and agendas. In many instances the omission of some facts or reporting one side of the issue is considered fair game. Allow me to share this example.

Sandra and I are both residents and taxpayers of the State of Georgia. I am sorry to say that at the time of this writing, the political party that favors the death of children through abortion currently holds power.

For more than a decade a simple bill, known as "A Woman's Right to Know" has been introduced and reintroduced in the Georgia legislature. I have watched this bill closely for over ten years while pro-life individuals tried to get it out of committee. And even now, the bill continues to be reintroduced. It has never made it out of committee, has never been given the opportunity to be voted on by the General Assembly.

This simple bill that keeps being reintroduced in the Georgia legislature would require a woman's referring physician or the doctor scheduled to perform an abortion procedure on her to provide her with six basic items of information at least twenty-four hours before the abortion procedure took place. These items include:

(1) The name of the doctor performing the abortion.

(2) The medical risks associated with the particular abortion procedure the doctor plans to use.

(3) The probable gestational age of the unborn child.

(4) The medical risks associated with carrying the child to term instead of proceeding with the abortion procedure.

(5) The medical assistance benefits that may be available for prenatal care of the unborn child;

(6) The fact that the father is liable to assist in the support of the child.

Supporters cannot get this simple and basic law passed in Georgia even though seventeen other sates have enacted this legislation.

The forces that work against such laws are truly amazing to watch. Opposition to such a law is openly led by paid lobbyists. They know when any such bill is going to be heard in committee before any "pro-life" supporters are informed.

When hearing meetings are scheduled, these opposition lobbyists are seated front and center in the hearing room. Their associates, those friendly to their cause, fill the rest of the room. At one such meeting there were only three "pro-lifers" able to make it into the hearing room. I know, because I was one of them.

I don't know what the influence is that creates and supports such a system, but it has worked effectively for more that a decade. You have to acknowledge their ability to manipulate the political process, and "John Q. Public" back home never suspects a thing.

One year post-abortion women came and lobbied the Georgia State Legislature in favor of "A Woman's Right to Know" legislation. They roamed the hallways of the state capitol and called on any senator or representative who they thought might listen to them. It was emotionally and physically draining for these women, but they didn't give up.

They begged for "A Woman's Right to Know". They explained the pain of living with making such a monumental decision with the little information given to women at abortion clinics now. They didn't want other women to suffer as they have suffered. But even with all their efforts, the bill was never brought out of committee to be voted upon.

You see, in a Georgia State legislature committee there is no mandatory recorded vote on any issue considered. Legislators can go back to their home districts and lead people to believe anything they want, because there is no proof either for or against them.

The fact is the actions of some Georgia state legislators are really nothing more than dirty little secrets that stay behind the closed doors of committee rooms during final wrangling and decisions. Such a system allows a legislator to remain in good standing with abortion supporting forces in the capital city of

Atlanta (where the abortion industry is strong and active), yet return back to their home districts throughout the state appearing as if they are a true "pro-family" elected official. They can run the roads back home presenting a "pro-family" image, then come to Atlanta and vote however the head of their political party tells them to vote so they can keep their prestige and power and take their share of "pork" back home.

Why would anyone be opposed to a bill that simply gives a woman about to undergo a serious medical procedure all the reasonable information she needs in order to make a complete and thorough decision? Make no mistake: if the governor or the lieutenant governor or the speaker of the house wanted such a bill to come out of committee, it would have years ago.

8

The Justices' Response

As we dress for dinner, Sandra is nervous about her appearance. She gets "butterflies" about speaking and feels the anxiety of getting her message across. There isn't one element of speaking in public that she enjoys.

She looks in the mirror a final time, combs her hair again and gives it a final touch of hair spray.

We go to meet our host for dinner. Sandra and I are introduced to those sponsoring this event. They are kind, gentle and dedicated. They too are frustrated with the response to their efforts to get the truth out about abortion. The simple fact that it is wrong to lie, to deceive and to manipulate women at any time, but especially when they are vulnerable. They are unwavering in their desire of "justice for all". And yet they are ridiculed and mislabeled and they're motives generalized to fit the stereotype of extremists and hate mongers. Hopefully our presence will encourage them to continue with their efforts to educate the general public that abortion scars women.

Sandra and I take our seat at the head table. Sandra carefully watches to see which fork to use. She is accustomed to simple fare and the place setting with its multiple forks and the 1000 people seated in front of us are intimidating. She endures the discomfort as she bares the undeserved guilt over her involvement in the court case, with a little shrug and a look in her eye that indicates "I don't want to disappoint anybody."

After all, the decision of whether or not to allow the elimination of a woman's unborn child would be a huge load for anyone to carry. The court's decision determined whether Sandra would end up getting shot at or not. The justice's decision determined whether she would live in fear for the rest of her life. Their response would influence how people would judge Sandra sight unseen. Passions from both sides of the abortion issue would be focused on Sandra once they discovered who she really was.

But how did the courts consider Sandra personally? In the *Doe v Bolton* case the United States Supreme Court issued a ruling that I still have trouble comprehending. The court plainly said,

> **"If the (original federal) court says the proffer of proof was unnecessary, then why do we need to be concerned about whether she (the plaintiff, "Mary Doe") is fictitious or a real person?"**

In other words, the justices of the U.S. Supreme Court didn't care who Sandra was. She didn't matter in their rule of law. The truth about her real case didn't matter to them. Her circumstances didn't matter. Desires didn't matter. Everything in the *Doe v Bolton* decision was based on the lower court's record, throughout the process judges were continually told lies and then based their decisions on the lies they were fed.

I can only wish that some judges from the federal court system were present. It would be justice if they could experience what Sandra's life has become. It would be justice if they received the same treatment that she has endured all these years. *Doe v. Bolton* was suppose to be a class action suit about pregnant women, but Sandra was the only pregnant woman named in the suit (hidden as "Mary Doe"). The rest were health professionals, physicians, nurses and counselors. All of them wanted abortion to be legal. All needed a desperate woman who would sign whatever papers were placed in front of her.

It didn't matter who she was or what she really wanted. It didn't matter to the U. S. Supreme Court if she was real or not. Sandra didn't matter. It didn't matter that she was just a poor woman asking for help in obtaining a divorce and regaining custody of her children.

When the Supreme Court ruling was announced Sandra was with her mother watching television. Her mother was ecstatic and told Sandra that she had changed the law. At that moment Sandra felt a great doom and weight come upon her shoulders. She still bears that guilt today.

I have seen how that weight has permeated every area of Sandra's life. I have seen her pain up close. As long as she is physically able she'll continue to speak out until her name is no longer associated with the killing of the unborn.

It is time for us to speak. We are given a warm introduction. We make our way to the podium and adjust our two microphones. I encourage her under my breath and look her in the eye to make sure she is ready.

As we stand before the crowded banquet audience I remind myself that I can never fully comprehend the pain or frustration Sandra has experienced. Although we have gone over and over exactly how this happened to her, a part of her will never understand. Sandra is afraid of the courts and believes the worst will happen if anything goes before a judge. She steadfastly believes the justice system works only for those with the most influence and money.

Sandra believes that others have found "Lady Justice" not only blind but also stone deaf and mute as far as their circumstances were concerned. Those vulnerable in our society too often watch from the sidelines while the rich and politically connected get the speedy trials and "special justice". Too often the winners are those who can hire the attorney that can best spin the truth and plant doubt. In Sandra's eyes, American Justice has become a debate club where justice and truth are not the primary goals, only winning the argument. The person with the most money hires the best debater and wins.

Even though she voices these thoughts she still believes with her whole heart that, eventually, the truth will stand, especially concerning her case. Otherwise, she wouldn't put herself through the ordeal of speaking tonight.

Sandra has an abiding faith in the power of Jesus Christ.

The assurance of His love overshadows all other knowledge in her life. This great love sustains her and gives her strength. Her belief is basic but unshakable. She believes with her whole being that someday the right person will listen to her story and come forward to right this great wrong. She doesn't know when or where, but she knows this in all certainly. Until that time, we'll continue to accept speaking engagements and endure the discomfort of travel.

9
The Absent Media

Everyone at this evening's banquet knows that no T. V. footage about this event will be seen on the nightly broadcast. Stories like ours are never considered important news. I have sadly learned from experience that in order to be promoted in today's media, an item has to be "politically correct," and those in control define what is and isn't politically correct. They do not believe our side of this controversial issue is worth hearing. Those who hold the power to "keep the public informed" will ignore Sandra's appearance.

I often watch news shows and read newspapers and news magazines that supposedly feature "investigative reporting". I think it is interesting how many times the number of blacks on death row is front-page news but the percentage of black children aborted is not considered "newsworthy"? Blacks in America now number roughly 12 percent of the population but account for more that 35 percent of all abortions. In my home state of Georgia 54 percent of the abortions performed last year were done on black women, ironically mostly by white doctors.

The vast majority of black political leaders in the state of Georgia and many of the black voters belong to a political party that for all intents and purposes are committing genocide on their race. Beautiful black babies are being eliminated at a faster rate than other babies. They don't seem to see any contradiction and no one appears to think this is newsworthy.

Where are the experiences of post-abortion women reported? I've never seen that as a topic on a talk show, a television news magazine or the headline of a supposedly "unbiased" investigative series. Both former workers from the abortion industry and women who have undergone abortions are more than willing to testify, to tell what they know. I have seen post-abortion women plead for someone, anyone who would listen to the truth of what happened to them. Some of the medical professionals who clean up the carnage are willing to speak. Why is this side of the abortion issue never covered by the media?

Only once have I experienced the frustration that Sandra lives with every day. I'll never forget that day, the day I learned that there is bias in the media. I realized there is a force that decides what is newsworthy and what is ignored depending on what is "politically correct".

The date was Thursday, January 22, 1998. Sandra and I were in Washington, D.C., to attend the annual March for Life, the massive "pro-life" rally held every year on the anniversary of the *Roe v. Wade* and *Doe v. Bolton* decisions. Nellie Gray and her volunteers have been staging this pro-life event every year since these decisions became law. She would not let the anniversary of this murderous decision pass without being remembered. Nellie and her volunteers work all year to plan, organize, and orchestrate the dinner and the march.

While many American cities hold their own March for Life events, the central one in Washington, D. C. is a huge celebration for life. Families from all over the U.S. come every year, no matter what the weather or inconvenience The children literally grow up with this event as part of their family history.

The 1998 program was very special, as it commemorated the 25th anniversary of the court decisions. Surely this time the media will listen, I kept telling myself. This time they will have to cover the story fairly. March for Life's 25th anniversary of *Roe v. Wade* and *Doe v Bolton* was just too well planned, too big of a story for the media to ignore. There were hundreds of people at the Rose Dinner and thousands at the March for Life. This landmark event featured the three main people who have had more to do with abortion that anyone in the United States. Dr. Bernard Nathanson was there. Norma McCorvey was there. And Sandra was there. All scheduled to speak. All ready to say they were "pro-life".

You can't ignore someone like Dr. Nathanson who for years ran the largest abortion clinic in the nation, in New York City. It was open for business 364 days a year, only closing its door for one day every twelve months. Dr. Nathanson coined the phrase "pro-choice" and "a woman's right to choose". He was there when the statistics of how many women died from illegal abortions were falsified. They were deliberately embellished and presented before the United States Supreme Court as the truth. These made up facts are part of the record of *Roe v. Wade*. But Dr. Nathanson could not live with the facts he came to know so well, the truth he could no longer deny. Not only did he stop performing abortions, Dr. Nathanson produced a powerful video entitled, "The Silent Scream" to show the world what a baby does as the abortion instruments approach the child in the womb. This video indisputably shows the baby realizes something is wrong and tries to get away from the invading object. It is not the peaceful end of the baby's life that woman have been led to believe. Dr. Nathanson was convinced that when Americans saw the video they would realize what abortion really was. He has converted to Catholicism and was there that day to share his story.

Norma McCorvey, better known by her court case name, "Jane Roe" of *Roe v. Wade,* was present. Norma has also experienced a religious conversion and is now actively "pro-life", telling the world at every opportunity that she is convinced abortion is the termination of a unique and irreplaceable life. She too was not given complete information regarding her court case. She has started the ministry "Roe No More" and works tirelessly to get her story out. She was ready to share her experience, who better than the woman whose name is most associated with abortion.

The third person, of course, was Sandra Cano. "Mary Doe" of *Doe v. Bolton* would once again tell the world that she never believed in abortion and never had an abortion. She would explain that her attorney did not carry out Sandra's desires in the courtroom, and that her case was based on lies and deceit.

So the 1998 March for Life had the three most publicly associated people concerning abortion there to firmly state their "pro-life" positions at the Rose Dinner the evening of the 25th anniversary of these monumental court decisions. Could there be a more perfect opportunity or better setting for the media to inform America about such an important time in the history of the United States?

We believed this 25th anniversary event was so important that Sandra and I spent two nights away from home instead of our usual one. She worried about her grandchildren terribly, but Sandra was determined to support this special event in every way she could. And with our high expectations, we made sure we were in our room to watch the news, to judge the quality of the coverage for ourselves.

But the lead stories on the major networks were not about the March for Life. None of their reporters covered the Rose Dinner speakers. As Sandra and I sat in out hotel room and switched to every channel, we did find two stories, over and over again. One dominated the news, and the other was the only coverage we could find related to the 25th anniversary of *Roe v. Wade and Doe v. Bolton*.

The main story was about Monica Lewinsky. The day we arrived for the March for Life event was the day the story broke about the White House intern sexually involved with the President of the United States. Well, you say, of course such a huge news story would overshadow an event that has taken place annually over the past twenty-five years. The only problem with such reasoning is that the media had not just found out about the problems with this presidential intern. The story had been ignored for months, some say for more than a year. Why was the decision made to broadcast the story on the 25th anniversary of *Roe v. Wade* and *Doe v. Bolton* decisions? By doing so the media was able to pigeonhole the March for Life event by claiming to have something bigger to cover instead.

As for the second story, the media showed Vice-President Al Gore across town attending the "pro-choice" dinner celebrating the 25th anniversary of legalized abortions. The "pro-choice" dinner was featured. The "pro-life" dinner with its three highly visible speakers was ignored. So much for "objectivity" by the media.

10
The Attendants

Some day there should be a special place in our history books for the individuals who work so hard to produce events like the March for Life. You have to admire these people for going forward year after year and not giving up, especially when you consider the odds that are against them. These people continue in their fight to remind the world that as Americans "we are endowed by our Creator with certain inalienable rights," and that the first of these rights is the right to life.

After all, if the people influencing the politicians and the news controllers can make the world think that a life is of no value then what is the next step. Is it too hard to carry that thought forward to where someone can argue that others may also not hold value to society ... those too sick ... those to old ... those in the wrong ethnic group ... those too religious ... or those not holding to the "right" religion? Who can determine when someone does not contribute enough to society, and should be denied their right to life? It happens every day, in abortion clinics across America.

"Pro-life" people are really fighting for all of us. Someday the world will see, but for now it is truly an uphill battle for these defenders of the unborn. After all some of their biggest opponents hold power in the media.

I look out over the crowd before us and wonder just who is listening to Sandra this time. Have they always been "pro-life" or are some seared by a personal abortion experience?

Abortion providers supply trained individuals who know just how to apply the proper pressure to get their desired result; another confused mentally manipulated woman; another aborted baby. The providers spread such lies as, "It's just like having your tonsils removed," or "It's no more than the cartilage in your ear," or "The fetus doesn't feel pain". Are those who have lived through this deception here for this meeting?

Some present claim to be pro-life Christians who vocally oppose abortion and speak against anyone involved in abortion procedures. But I know of some who didn't keep to their spoken convictions when their daughter became the victim of an unwanted pregnancy. They quickly and quietly had their daughters take advantage of the abortion procedures they speak against now. Hypocrisy can abound when an issue hits too close to home.

Will such a family live the rest of their lives holding onto the lie that, "If the neighbors don't find out, then it's as if the pregnancy never happened. Our family is pro-life, don't you dare tell anyone we took you to a clinic." Betrayed by her own family, the woman is left to bear the loneliness, the guilt and the regret. The child is never to be mentioned again and the young woman has no one with whom to share her thoughts. Are such people here to listen to Sandra's story?

I see many men in the audience. Are any of them recalling a time when they forced a wife, a sister, a daughter or a lover to have an abortion? This so-called "great feminist victory" has reduced the responsibility of fathers to a few hundred dollars and a ride to a clinic. Some men actually claim to believe that such an offer somehow absolves them of their responsibility to both the woman and the child. His life goes on unaffected, the abortion is a quick fix to any pending financial or social responsibility. Sandra is about to start telling her story. Are these men listening?

Many women are present. How will Sandra's story affect them? Throughout America, especially inside abortion clinics, women are not told the risks of an abortion procedure, such as the increased chances of later miscarriages, breast cancer or sterility. Women are never told of the sensation they will experience when the tiny life they carry is removed. Later in life they describe the experience as an actual loss of part of themselves physically, mentally and emotionally. They are never the same.

Are there women present who have had an abortion? If so, will Sandra's story dig up memories they have tried so hard to put behind them? What mind games must these women play in order to bear the consequences of their abortion?

So many women who have undergone abortions now routinely state that they are left with feelings of guilt, condemnation and self-loathing. These women are haunted by thoughts like, "How could I not know it was a baby?" or "He didn't love me enough to want his child and stand by me." And then there is the mystery of what the child would have looked like and what he or she could have become. The ache of wanting to let the child know, "I loved you, and I still love you. I'm so sorry. Please forgive me."

Of course, not all women who have undergone an abortion experience these emotions. Some are in very deep denial. I believe, some would even destroy their "unwanted" born children if it were legal. They could strap them in a car and watch it roll in a lake or systematically drown them in their own bathroom or throw them in the trash once they are born. After all, isn't that what legalized abortion does, just before birth instead of after"? Isn't it supposed to be a quick fix, a solution to a problem pregnancy, an unwanted life?

Abortion supporters claim their position provides the answer for such chilling statements as, "A pregnancy at this time would ruin your life." Or "What about your career, your college degree. These are more important at this time." Or what about, "It would destroy your parents if they knew you'd gotten pregnant." And then there's, "This pregnancy can be taken care of quickly and quietly and no one will ever know. You can spare everyone if you just go forward with this procedure." As a result of following this logic, millions of women are carrying a pain so horrific and so penetrating that they dare not speak about abortion, lest the memories, fears and emotions overwhelm them. The secret remains a closed door in their mind and soul, and few want to open it.

Sandra shares the burden of these women. She blames herself for being used in the court proceedings that have allowed abortion to be declared legal. Sandra believes that her case made women fair game for the mental manipulation these women have endured. That's why she is here, to let them know she was used as they were. She never wanted her case to be a landmark anything, just a routine divorce.

11
Deliberate Deception

Sandra and I begin by explaining why there are two of us behind the podium. The fact that Sandra is much more comfortable with a question and answer format. She doesn't worry about her thoughts rambling or about having to think too far ahead. We will be reviewing what we went over on the plane. If something is omitted or not covered with the proper detail we can go back over it. They will experience her personality more if she is relaxed. Our goal to have them appreciate Sandra for who she is and what she has been through.

We cover her humble childhood, her marriage and the circumstances that caused her to go to Atlanta legal aid. We get to the Supreme Court case and I am deeply concerned that the audience will not grasp this information. Here is the proof that Sandra's facts never changed but her lawyer, Pitts Hames told completely different versions of Sandra's actions.

In the Supreme Court transcript Pitts Hames stated that;

"She applied to the public hospital for an abortion,

where she was eligible for free medical care. Her application there was denied. She later applied, through a private physician, to a private hospital abortion committee, where her abortion application was approved. Her — she did not obtain the abortion, however, because She did not have the cash to deposit and pay her hospital bill in advance.

The truth is far different. Quite simply these events never occurred. Sandra never applied to the public hospital for an abortion. Her application was never denied because her application never existed. She never requested for a private physician to submit an abortion application on her behalf. These statements are a complete fabrication on Pitts Hames part to make her desire for abortion on demand legal. How do we know this?

Pitts Hames is betrayed by her own words. After Sandra got her records unsealed in 1988, interest in the story was directed not only to Sandra but to her attorney, Margie Pitts Hames, as well. Pitts Hames was interviewed and her version of events appeared in the Fulton Daily Report, a legal newspaper in Atlanta. There she revealed that an abortion had been scheduled for Sandra at a private hospital, Georgia Baptist. The cost of the procedure was taken care of for Sandra. **"As for the hospital bill. Sandra's lawyers raised money to cover it."** Also according to the article, Dr. Donald Block volunteered to perform the abortion for free. This is the same doctor who delivered Sandra's first three children. He would eliminate the fourth at no charge.

The revealing thing about this recollection is that it contradicts the argument Pitts Hames made to the United States Supreme Court. Remember she stated before the justices that Sandra applied to a private hospital for an abortion and that the application for abortion was approved but "**she did not obtain the abortion, however, because she didn't have the cash to deposit and pay her hospital bill in advance**". The truth of why Sandra didn't go ahead with the abortion is quite different than what the court was led to believe.

So what did happen? Yes, an abortion was scheduled for Sandra. Without Sandra's will or consent the lawyer and Sandra's mother had planned to eliminate the child. Sandra found out about the plan the night before she was to enter the hospital. She fled to Oklahoma by bus to save the life of her child.

Sandra believes that the Supreme Court was deliberately deceived. Things that Sandra had no knowledge of, and never consented to, were presented as actual events. There were two miscarriages of justice. The first was Dorothy T. Beasley's statements concerning the lack of evidence "**we know of no facts about her at all**" "**There are no facts in this case**" "**It is not a complete divulgence of the facts surrounding her circumstances.**" "**We know no facts about her at all.**" "**No interrogatories were answered, no proof was submitted.**" The second was the lies that were presented to the justices as truth. Once again what Sandra wanted didn't matter. The true facts didn't matter. Sandra believes Pitts Hames had a goal and nothing would stand in her way. The tools used to accomplish this goal were lies and deception brought before the highest court in America.

12
Reason For Her Resolve

Near the end of Sandra's presentation is where she has the most difficulty emotionally. Sometimes she is unable to go on and I have to finish for her. When she was first relating her life's story to me, this is the only time she wept.

After her records were unsealed in 1988 there was much publicity that caused Sandra to be reunited with the daughter she had placed for adoption, the child who was the center of the Supreme Court action. Sandra took her daughter and grandchildren into her life and home.

Shortly afterwards, while standing on her front porch holding a grandchild in her arms, Sandra was shot at, the bullet coming close to striking both Sandra and the baby. Fearing for her life and the lives of her family, Sandra decided to give up public life and "go underground". She might have remained that way living in fear of being discovered again, and her story might have ended there. But Cory changed everything.

Sandra's newly found daughter gave birth to Cory on April

26, 1992, twenty-two years to the day after the filing of the *Doe v. Bolton* case. Cory was premature, according to his birth certificate he was only 28 weeks old and 9 inches in length, weighing 9.4 ounces. Although he was a perfectly formed baby boy, his lungs were not developed enough to sustain life. Sandra and her daughter watched as Cory fought for every breath, he only lived a few hours.

Through those hours, the nurse on duty never referred to Cory as anything more than a "fetus". Cory was given no medical aid. He was simply allowed to die.

Sandra realized something that afternoon. Cory was considered nothing more than a "fetus" because of her Supreme Court case. And babies bigger than Cory were dying every day because of her case. Some are full term. In the procedure known as "partial birth abortion" the baby is delivered feet first and stabbed in the back of the head with scissors, the child's brain is suctioned out before the head leaves the mother.

All because of Sandra's case all because she was used and the facts were not important. Has she become angry and bitter? No, she is Sandra. She tries to do the right thing and tries to please. At one point she lived in an apartment where the residents were mostly Spanish speaking. Some were in this country legally and some illegally. Their children didn't know about Easter baskets so she used $200 of her $900 disability check to buy them all Easter baskets. She is raising two grandchildren with this money and the funds were not discretionary by any means. She needed the money for her basic living expenses but wanted the apartment children to experience the joy in Easter. These children were not all planned. They weren't from two-parent households. Some don't even know their fathers. There isn't enough money for all these children's basic needs. None of these things mattered to Sandra. The only thing that mattered to Sandra was that they were children whom she wanted to show love and kindness. To have this unselfish, loving grandmother carry the responsibility of the killing of children is so unjust.

At this point in our presentation, Sandra sometimes becomes so overcome with emotion that I have to finish for her. But Cory set Sandra's resolve. His life, though brief, changed Sandra forever. No matter what, she will continue in her effort to have America know the truth.

13

Connecting With The Hurting

We work together to complete Sandra's presentation. After we close and the master of ceremonies makes the usual re-marks and comments, people come to speak with Sandra. Some clasp her hand and offer support. I once saw a woman remove her religious medal from her own neck to give to Sandra for comfort. Sandra was deeply moved. On the trip home she held the medal and marveled at the woman's thoughtfulness. Some come with tears in their eyes to offer sympathy that she was treated so unjustly by the courts. Some come to have their photo taken with her.

And then there are those at the edge of the crowd. I thought some of them might be with us this evening. And they are. It seems they always are. They come forward when the others have left. They are the women scarred by abortion.

These women live with the fact that some people will never understand how they could have undergone such a procedure.

They always expect to hear condemning comments such as, "How could you not know it was a baby?" or "Surely you must have known what you were going to do was wrong." They expect to be rejected by people who can not comprehend the pressure that led to their vulnerability so they wait for the others to leave first. Their actions that fateful day, when they were so desperate, remain unknown to others for fear of ridicule, and to keep their own self-loathing hidden.

They come forward quietly. They share what women aren't told before an abortion procedure. Once again I hear them say things we've heard before in different cities. "They never told me my baby would feel pain." "They told me it was no more than the cartilage in my ear." "They didn't tell me that my baby girl had brainwaves and fingerprints." "They never told me of the sensation that I would feel when the life was removed from my body, or that the same feeling would engulf me with the same intensity every time the procedure was remembered." "They never told me about the nightmares." "They never told me of the depression that I would experience every year on the anniversary of that event." "They never told me how hard the secret would be to carry." "I can not pretend that it never happened."

I hear those comments so often, as I stand beside Sandra. I hear their voices and hope in someway that we've made them feel less alone and given them the hope that in the future other women will not be treated as they were. Just as the judicial process manipulated Sandra, clinic personnel manipulated these women.

These women share so many of the same things. There's always the burden of the secret. Some anxiety of, "The friend who took me to the clinic knows, but will she keep the secret?" "They never told me how to tell my current husband. When you first meet a man, you don't tell him. Later, as you get to know him and realize you want to share your life, how do you tell him?" "How do I tell my children? If they knew, would they ever see me in the same way again?" "Will this one event that influences every other area of my life remain a secret?" "They never told me at the clinic how complicated the "simple procedure" makes your life."

Some of these women tell us they have even asked women to go with them while they tell their husband that they are post-abortion, because they just couldn't face him alone. I've yet to hear a "happy" story about abortion. I have yet to hear the clinics give a response that has satisfied these women's tortured souls.

On average it takes two years of counseling for a post-abortion woman to come out of such a tormented life. That's two years of struggling and dealing with the results of an abortion procedure after years of denial.

Post-abortion women regularly deny the connection between eating disorders and abortion, between a promiscuous life-style and abortion, between attempted suicide and abortion, between the fear of intimate relationships and abortion. Some are left facing how abortion left them physically as well as emotionally.

14
A Place For Healing

There is one place where the secret is revealed. The naked truth of the abortion experience is faced head on. I've witnessed women come out of the denial with a sorrowful dignity. They can finally mourn the little person they've tried to ignore for so many years. This place of restoration and healing is called the "National Memorial for the Unborn".

It is in Chattanooga, Tennessee. My husband, Bryan and I first learned of the Memorial when we were asked to help Sandra with her role in their dedication ceremony. The "National Memorial for the Unborn" is the site of a former abortion clinic purchased by "pro-life" supporters.

The abortion clinic opened in 1975. One-half of the building housed the actual abortion chambers. In its years of operation, 35,000 lives were lost in those rooms. Ten years after the abortion clinic opened, a small group of Christians rented an office in the building just across the street from the abortion clinic. There they established AAA Women's Services, a crisis pregnancy center. They were joined and supported over the following years by those desiring to assist women in a crisis pregnancy and help save children. Together with individuals from various church denominations and pro-life activists, they formed the Pro-Life Majority Coalition of Chattanooga (ProMaCC) in 1999.

Within the span of two years, the co-owners of the abortion clinic, both women in their fifties, were diagnosed with cancer and died. The commercial landlord who had leased out the building to the abortion clinic was forced to file for bankruptcy. Word of the impending sale of the building containing the abortion clinic was passed along to the ProMaCC coalition members with only four day remaining to enter a bid.

Before the deadline the coalition put together $300,000 to bid towards the purchase of the property containing the abortion clinic. The main opponent to the coalition in the bidding was the abortion doctor, but the abortionist dropped out of the bankruptcy auction when the coalition bid reached $294,000.

As the new owners ProMaCC was able to evict the abortionist, since the clinic's lease had expired two days before the sale papers were signed. Half of the building was remodeled to provide a center of support for women dealing with a crisis pregnancy.

The other half of the building, which had contained the abortion chambers, was demolished with a bulldozer. In the ruins the next morning a neatly placed little teddy bear was found. Someone had come in the night and left it. A memorial was built on this site to remember those valuable lost lives, and to recognize the grief carried by the millions of living victims of abortion.

The "National Memorial for the Unborn" is a fifty-foot long granite wall, which holds memorial plaques ordered from forty-seven states throughout America. These plaques bear names, dates and messages expressing in inadequate words the outpouring of grieving hearts.

This memorial site provides a tangible and accessible place for people to express grief and remembrance. And people come; all sorts of people come. Grandparents come to acknowledge the grandchild they will never hold. Fathers come, some who wanted the baby, but their desires were determined "immaterial" to the wishes of the mother and/or those putting pressure on her to eliminate the baby. Other fathers come to try and get over the guilt of giving a woman in their life the unfair ultimatum of, "Kill it or I'll leave". Family members come who wished they had intervened to save the life of a child they now will never know.

Most moving of all are the mothers of the aborted children that come to this place. Over and over, on the brass plaques that are composed by individuals and placed on the wall, and in letters to the aborted children left on the ledge, one reads, "Please forgive me." "I'm so sorry." "I'll hold you in heaven."

I have taken post-abortion women to the memorial. When they first experience the memorial site they are engulfed in regret and sorrow. But as we stand there and they read the letters and the plaques from other post-abortion women, they are fortified with the realization that they are no longer alone. The emotional toll and energy that was extracted feeling shame is replaced with a quest for truth and justice. They are renewed to fight against the manipulation of women and to end legalized abortion on demand, to no longer live a lie or have the truth of what living with the secret of an abortion is like hidden and denied in their mind.

On some days the guilt these women suffer seems bigger than life. But on other days the factors that worked against them help relieve the guilt they carry. Days like when they visit this memorial.

When these post-abortion women unite ... and they will ... when their truth is known ... and it will be ... the legislative, executive and judicial systems will have to act. The simple questions of "Is this a separate human being?" will be addressed. The basic DNA evidence used by agents of many courts today will have to be applied.

During the argument in *Doe v. Bolton* heard before the Supreme Court Wednesday, October 11, 1972, one of the justices actually compared an abortion to a tonsillectomy. And I quote **"But you wouldn't contend, would you, that the State would have authority to enact a statue or sustain a statute that would forbid tonsillectomies, for example?"**

No longer will that argument be a substitution for scientific evidence. Once basic DNA evidence, the type regularly used in other court cases, is applied to abortion cases judges will have to face the truth. Science, logic and common sense will someday enter this arena of lies, deception and manipulation. I firmly believe that with all my heart.

15
The Providers

Shouldn't it be wrong to manipulate a woman at the most vulnerable time in her life? Shouldn't women have the same legal protection and rights during this medical procedure as during adoption, when full medical disclosure and a complete review of all the rights and options available must be given and understood before final action can occur?

Even if a woman abuses her child, the parent-child relationship has legal protection and legal recourse before the relationship can be terminated. Shouldn't it be wrong to permit a woman to make an irreversible decision with insufficient information.

Some abortion providers have left the industry. Some were the owners of clinics, some were the doctors who performed the abortions, some were the counselors who talked to the girls and some were the medical assistants whose job it was to make sure all of the baby was removed from the womb. They are willing to speak about their experiences, what they saw, and what they did. I have heard their stories on more than one occasion.

It is not easy for these individuals to relive their roles in the "pro-choice" movement. But their desire for the world to know the truth is greater than the pain of facing the damage they caused.

At a convention in Chicago, former abortion providers shared their experiences as the video "Meet the Abortion Providers," was made. It is available through the Pro-Life Action League, (offices in Chicago, IL). This video along with other videos and written testimonies are a window into the abortion industry that presents a picture they certainly don't volunteer.

For starters, I was shocked to learn from these people, that they and their former co-workers used to laugh behind closed doors at the term "pro-choice". There was no "choice" given by the "counselors" at their abortion clinics. The only "choice" concerned which clinic a woman would use for their abortion procedure.

I am told that in such "counseling sessions" all focus is taken off the baby and put instead on some trivial expectation. For example, a teenage girl may be told, "If you have a baby, you won't be able to be a cheerleader, you won't be able to enter a beauty pageant." What kind of logic is that, on one side cheerleading, on the other the destiny of a unique, irreplaceable human being?

What happens with that "logic" after the young woman undergoes an abortion procedure? These women have come forward with notarized affidavits stating they have redefined themselves and their self-image. Motivated by self-loathing they become promiscuous sometimes ending up having multiple abortions. They never become a beauty queen or cheerleader because of the emotional pain caused by their abortion.

Former abortion providers have admitted that their clinics, intentionally, prescribed the lowest dose birth control pill. Without informing the patient, the pill would have a 30% failure rate. The result was repeat business.

Some former providers say their clinics treated women for venereal disease without informing their patients that the antibiotics prescribed would negate the effects of their birth control medication. The outcome? Another 10 to 15 percent repeat business rate from the women who had supposedly been "helped" by the clinic they trusted.

If abortion is so right, why do post-abortion women and former abortion providers feel so bad? Why are these former clinic workers now so horrified about the work they did?

I have learned abortion clinic workers are taught to deny the existence of "post-abortion syndrome". If a woman who underwent an abortion procedure calls the clinic back asking about her nightmares or depression, she is told that she must have had such problems before the abortion took place.

One former clinic director came to the sad realization that abortion is not about helping women but about greed. She regularly encountered providers who didn't care about the woman and didn't care about the baby or the undeniable fact that "so many women are dying" following legal abortion procedures. This director found her conscience would no longer permit her participation and she quit.

In 1997 in the United States, there were 1,186,039 legal abortions reported to the Federal Center for Disease Control. Using an average cost per abortion of $450 that means the abortion industry generated $1,462,050 each day in 1997 alone. That is $533,648,250 a year. Eliminating the unborn is a very profitable endeavor.

People who perform abortion procedures consistently deny any damage to post-abortion women, physically or emotionally. These women are left alone with their fears. I know. I have listened to them tell Sandra and me their stories.

Pro-choice supporters are right about one thing. Abortion is about women. Only the supporters and advocates promoting abortion focus on their cause. What is in the woman's best interest, complete information, is never considered.

How sad that these women are alone with the fear that their husbands will leave them if they learn about the abortion. So they keep the knowledge to themselves, even if the abortion took place before their marriage. These women fear their children may end up hating them if they learn about their mother's abortion experience. They even fear the judgment of their friends if they confide in them about an abortion and seek comfort for the struggles they now silently battle.

Most sad to me are the post-abortion women who fear the condemnation of their churches if anyone learns they underwent an abortion procedure, regardless of how long ago it happened. I have seen how a relationship with Christ has brought comfort and healing to Dr. Nathanson, Norma McCorvey, and Sandra Cano. The simple fact that God loves me brings peace. Because of Christ's sacrifice God, in His great love, has forgiven me. God is giving me the strength to face each day. I pray they will all experience that comfort someday.

For now these women are isolated, guilty and abandoned. They think their experience is safely locked away. But the truth keeps surfacing again and again, with great remorse. They feel pressure from (family, lover, counselor etc.) to keep quiet. As long as they remain quiet there is no threat to the powers that put them in this cauldron. The women are left to bear these scars alone for the rest of their lives. But the truth will always stand and a legal effort is under way to overturn *Roe v. Wade* and *Doe v. Bolton*.

Allan Parker, CEO and Founder of the Justice Foundation (www.TxJF.org) is representing Sandra Cano and Norma McCorvey. There is now a legal opportunity for all post-abortion women and people who stand with them to be able to have their truth known in court. The Justice Foundation is working with Harold Cassidy and the National Foundation for Life (www.NFFLLP.org.) in an endeavor to obtain affidavits to take into court. In these affidavits women will have their "day in court". The following are some of the question these women are asked to answer.

Were you adequately informed of the nature of abortion, what it is what it does?

Were you adequately informed of the consequences of abortion?

Did anyone pressure you into having an abortion? If so, who?

Were you informed of any link between abortion and breast cancer?

Have you had breast cancer?

How has your abortion affected you?

Based on your own experience, what would you tell a court that believes abortion should be legal?

Would there be a need for such questions if the procedure were anything but abortion? A television commercial for a prescription medicine contains more information and warning than these women received in their entire abortion process.

Finally a chance to be heard. I believe that these organizations will persevere. In the end the courts will decide the abortion issue based on fact and testimony. I believe the U. S. Supreme Court will rectify the way *Doe v. Bolton* was heard. This time it will matter that the people represented in the cases are real.

For more information on this court proceeding or to learn how anyone can stand with these women, please contact: *The Justice Foundation, 8122 Datapoint Drive, San Antonio, TX 78229 (210) 614-7151* or log on to www.operationoutcry.org

Sandra and I return to our room emotionally spent, moved by the women's pain and deeply humbled that Sandra's story brought them comfort.

We will catch a few hours sleep before returning to our homes. It is both an honor and responsibility when someone like Sandra has given you their trust. Bryan and I don't want to do anything that would let her down.

Sandra has been hurt and used so many times. And until more Americans know the facts behind Sandra's case ... I will again set my alarm for 5 A.M. You see. We always need extra time at the airport.

As I am finishing this manuscript the United States is still reeling from the events of September 11, 2001 and its wanton destruction. Nearly 3,000 precious lives were lost at the World Trade Center alone. President Bush has rightly declared war on terrorism and more than 85% of Americans support him in this decision. Yet every day more than 3,000 innocent, helpless babies die from legalized abortion in the United States. When will the war against them end? Speak up, you can help put an end to these senseless acts of terrorism.

Sybil J. Lash

© 2002

Sybil J. Lash and her husband, Bryan, did extensive research on Sandra's story and produced the video, "The High Courts Low Blow to Doe" which is available through Sentinel Productions, P.O. Box 1509, Lawrenceville, GA 30046-1509. They have been married for 33 years and have two married daughters and two granddaughters. Sybil has been an Aide to Georgia State Representative Mitchell Kaye of the 37th District and she is a recipient of the Eagle Forum "Eagle of the Year" award. She is also a Charter member North Atlanta Conservative Republican Women, the Gwinnett County Christian Coalition and a member of Georgia Right to Life.

Information

To help overturn Roe v. Wade and Doe v. Bolton and or to fill out either a Friend of the Court statement or post-abortion affidavit:

"Operation Outcry"
The Justice Foundation
8122 Datapoint, Suite 812
San Antonio, Texas 78229

210-614-7157
210-614-6656 FAX
www.operationoutcry.org

To obtain a copy of <u>"Meet the Abortion Providers"</u>
Pro-Life Action League
Joseph Scheidler
6160 North Cicero, Room # 600
Chicago, Illinois 60646

773-777-2900

To obtain Dr. Nathanson's video <u>" The Silent Scream"</u>
Pro-Life Action League
6160 North Cicero
Chicago, Illinois 60646

773-777-2900

To obtain the video about Sandra Cano entitled <u>"The High Court's Low Blow to Doe"</u>
Sentinel Productions
Post Office Box 1509
Lawrenceville, Georgia 30046

770-978-2350
770-736-7830

Appendix

Oral Arguments from Doe v. Bolton

U. S. Supreme Court   No. 70-40

Transcribed from audio tape

In The Supreme Court
Of The United States

— — — — — — — — — — — — —

No. 70-40

MARY DOE, et al., Appellants,

v.

ARTHUR K. BOLTON, Attorney

General of the State of Georgia, et al., Appellees.

— — — — — — — — — — — — —

Washington, D.C.,

Monday, December 13, 1971.

The above-entitled matter came on for argument
at 11:12 o'clock, a.m.

BEFORE:

WARREN E. BURGER, Chief Justice of the United States

WILLIAM O. DOUGLAS, Associate Justice

WILLIAM J. BRENNAN, JR., Associate Justice

POTTER STEWART, Associate Justice

BYRON R. WHITE, Associate Justice

THURGOOD MARSHALL, Associate Justice

HARRY A. BLACKMUN, Associate Justice

APPEARANCES:

MRS. MARGIE PITTS HAMES, Suite 822, 15 Peachtree St.,
N.E., Atlanta, Georgia 30303, for the Appellants.

MRS. DOROTHY T. BEASELY, 132 State Judicial Building,
40 Capitol Square, S. W., Atlanta, Georgia 30334,
for the Appellees.

CONTENTS

ORAL ARGUMENT OF:

Mrs. Margie Pitts Hames, for the Appellants

Mrs. Dorothy T. Beasley, for the Appellees

PROCEEDINGS

MR. CHIEF JUSTICE BERGER: We will hear arguments next in
No. 40, Mary Doe against Bolton.

Mrs. Hames, you may proceed whenever you're ready.

ORAL ARGUMENT OF MRS. MARGIE PITTS HAMES,

ON BEHALF OF THE APPELLANTS

MRS. HAMES: Mr. Chief Justice, and may it please the Court:

This is an appeal from the decision of the Northern District of Georgia, also a three-judge court, which declared portions of the Georgia abortion statute unconstitutional.

It upheld certain procedural requirements and refused to issue an injunction in support of the declaratory judgement.

The parties here include: Mary Doe, a pregnant woman, a married pregnant woman; doctors, nurses, ministers, social workers, and family planning and abortion counseling organizations.

They filed this action as a class action, seeking to represent members of their various classes.

The District Court below found that the right of privacy included the right to terminate an unwanted pregnancy, and that the statute which limited the reasons therefore was unduly restricted and overly broad.

The District Court found that Mary Doe and her class was entitled to declaratory relief. The positions, even though they were found to have standing, and other parties, were said to have insufficient collision of interests. This question we brought to this Court also.

This case stands, on jurisdictional grounds, similar to the Roe vs. Wade case, which has just been argued, except that no plaintiff in this case has pending criminal prosecutions outstanding against them.

It is our position that the jurisdiction of this Court is much like the case of Wisconsin vs. Constantineau, where, in that case — the statute in that case operated against a third party's rights:

Q   Excuse me.   These are class actions, too?

MRS. HAMES: Yes, Your Honor, they are. The statute in Wisconsin vs. Constantineau operated against a third party's rights, and I am sure you will recall that was the posting of the alcoholic case. The criminal penalty there ran against the bartender who sold alcoholic beverages. So that the woman - - the posted party would never have an opportunity to assert her rights - - it was a woman in the case - - in the defense of the criminal action against the bartender.

Here we have a like situation of the third party's rights, Mary Doe, who would never have an opportunity, we say, adequately to assert her constitutional rights in the defense of the doctor's criminal prosecution.

Georgia, like Texas, it is not a crime for a woman to submit to an abortion or to abort herself.

Q   Could she be guilty of a conspiracy to perform an abortion?

MRS. HAMES: I cannot cite you a case expressly, but it is my recollection that the Georgia courts have hold that she would not be so guilty. Her husband or her paramour could - -

Q   Might be.

MRS. HAMES: - - have been charged; but that, to my recollection, there has not been a charge brought against a woman as a conspirator.

Q   Mrs. Hames, the hospital here was not named as a defendant, was it?

MRS. HAMES: No, Your Honor, it was not.

Q   Is there a reason for that?

MRS. HAMES: The hospital was not thought to be an indispensable party, since the hospital abortion committee was a statutory committee, created by the statute, of the abortion statute. It was our opinion that under the Georgia law, dealing with the Attorney General and his powers, which gave him powers over all boards, committees, and commissions, as to matters of law, that this was sufficient to bring that interest into operation.

Also, the abortion committee is a revolving committee, and it would have involved various doctors from time to time. Most hospitals in Georgia have their various staff members sit on the abortion committee, so that it changes from month to month, or from day to day, even.

So that it was felt that bringing the Attorney General, the State Attorney General in as the defendant in the case would be sufficient to reach this State statutory abortion committee, in the exercise of the statutory authority given to them.

Mary Doe was a 22-year-old woman; she was married, and pregnant at the time this action was filed. Her reasons for abortion were several; she had three previous children, two of whom had been taken from her custody by State authorities because of her inability to care for them; and the third she had placed with adoptive parents at birth.

She applied to the public hospital for an abortion, where she was eligible for free medical care. Her application there was denied. She later applied, through a private physician, to a private hospital abortion committee, where her abortion application was approved.

Her — she did not obtain the abortion, however, because she did not have the cash to deposit and pay her hospital bill in advance. The Georgia statute is - -

Q   Is there a real Mary Doe, or is this just - -

MRS. HAMES: Yes, Your Honor, there is. And filed in the original files, which has been sent up to this Court; is a sealed affidavit which is signed in Mary Doe's real name. It was signed and filed with the court originally in the proceedings. She was present at the hearing in this case, and we offered to have her testify and disclose her identity and the court did not deem that necessary.

We filed in the fictitious name to protect her identity and avoid embarrassment. But that original affidavit is on file in this Court.

Q   I notice in the record that the State has removed her other three children, or at least two of them, from her custody because she's unable to care for them. Was that over her objections or with her consent, or just no opposition?

MRS. HAMES: It was not with her consent, Your Honor, as I recall; it was for the protection of her children.

Q   But removed under the broad welfare provision?

MRS. HAMES: Yes, Your Honor. Yes, Mr. Chief Justice.

Our major contention here, our appeal here is directed primarily at the procedural requirements left standing by the District Court below. Our statute does provide that rape is grounds for abortion; also fetal malformation and danger to the life of the woman, or serious permanent injury to her health.

These were the reasons that the court declared unconstitutional, finding that there were other good reasons, good and sufficient reasons for an abortion.

The requirements that are left standing are the residency requirement, that the woman's doctor have at least two consultants, who concur in his opinion, and approval by a hospital abortion committee, of at least three more doctors. And the accredited, licensed hospital provision; this accreditation requirement is by the Joint Commission on Hospital Accreditation of Chicago, Illinois, Corporation, which is a private organization.

There were other many reporting requirements, and miscellaneous provisions left in the statute; but I wish to direct the Court's attention to these, the hospital abortion committee, the accreditation residency requirement.

It is the appellants' contention that it's not necessary to debate the fetal life problem in this case, because, as the District Court below recognized, this statute is aimed at protecting the health of women. Judge Smith, in delivering the opinion of the court, found that the whole thrust of the present Georgia statute is to treat the problem as a medical one.

The only compelling State interest, however, that has been asserted by the State, is the interest in preserving fetal life. And in taking this approach to the statute, the State finds itself in a very inconsistent position, we feel; that is, of claiming that fetuses, from the moment of conception have the right to develop and be born, and yet, having abandoned such right as to these fetuses, the product of rape, which may likely be malformed, or those which may endanger the life or health of the women.

Further, the State is in the inconsistent position of financing a family planning program, which daily distributes - - excuse me?

Q   Under this statute, the fetus that's a product of rape, may that be aborted?

MRS. HAMES: Yes, Your Honor.

Q   Without more?

MRS. HAMES: I'm sorry?

Q   Without more, whether or not it's involving health of the mother?

MRS. HAMES: That's correct. Rape, both forcible and statutory; which is girls 13 years and younger in Georgia.

Q   That's by specific provision, I gather?

MRS. HAMES: Yes, that's one of the exceptions. Our law is modeled after the Model Penal Code, American Law Institute version.

The further inconsistency involves the financing of the family planning program, which distributes, through the Department of Public Health, the intra-uterine contraceptive device, which, substantial medical opinion shows, destroys the product of conception, or prevents implantation of the fertilized egg or embryo.

We feel that if the State has such an unfettered interest in fetal life, that these are very inconsistent positions.

Thus, it is our contention that the statute must be viewed as a health-of-the-woman directed-purpose statute.

I would point out that abortion is not a new medical procedure. Of course we've heard a lot about it in the last few years. But it's one that's been extensively performed throughout the history of our country, and of course illegally.

Because of the abortion statutes, the great majority of abortions have been performed by unskilled persons, those least equipped to take care of the health problems. Doctors, because it is a crime, have not been performing abortions.

Abortion statutes, however, have not stopped the abortions. They have not served a purpose, or they have not - - are not reaching the purpose of protecting fetal life. If that is a valid purpose.

To assume that these statutes do protect fetal life is to ignore the actual facts. In our brief, and in the many amici briefs filed in this case, there is extensive citation to statistics about illegal abortions, and the admission of patients for aseptic abortions, that is the incomplete abortions, into our hospitals, which show that illegal abortions are being performed.

What we're actually talking about is getting abortion out of the illegal arena into the health service arena, and this is the purpose of this litigations.

I would point out that illegal abortion and the complications therefrom is the largest single cause of maternal mortality in the United States. Therefore, abortion statutes have resulted in one of our nation's largest health problems.

It is our contention that the procedural requirement left

standing by the court below has virtually manipulated out of existence the right to terminate an unwanted pregnancy, as recognized by the Court.

The decision below characterizes the decision to terminate an unwanted pregnancy as a personal-medical decision. In commenting about the procedural requirements, the hospital abortion committee, the limitation to the accredited hospital, the court said that the State has an interest in the quality of health care, to be administered to its citizens; but this is not to imply that the present procedures are the best means of control. The present seems to be unnecessarily cumbersome and possibly a due process hazard. This was the observation of the court in a footnote. And it is our contention that these procedures are so cumbersome, costly and time-consuming as to have denied Mary Doe and members of her class, and doctors and members of their class, of their various rights.

Of course, there is an inherent time factor in pregnancy, and this must be a factor considered.

First trimester abortions are safer than late abortions.

Therefore, it is imperative that the right to terminate an unwanted pregnancy be efficiently exercised.

Mortality and complications for late abortions are three times
greater, after 12 weeks; and it is only about the sixth or eighth
week that pregnancy tests actually become accurate, or the degree
of accuracy is such that can reasonably predict whether one is
pregnant or not.

So that we actually have about 12 weeks - -

Q   Does the record disclose that?

MRS. HAMES: Does the record - - I'm sorry?

**Q   Does the record disclose that it is medically
established that pregnancy tests are not very accurate
until after six weeks?**

MRS. HAMES: No, Your Honor, we were not permitted to
introduce our evidence at the hearing, that was - - we had many
witnesses to testify about the various aspects of abortion and
pregnancy. I'm sure that this Court can take judicial notice of
many medical treatises which would disclose that this is a fact.

Q   Well, I'm asking if it is an established medical fact?

MRS. HAMES: Yes, it is my understanding that this is accepted procedure, that a pregnancy is not easily detectable until after the sixth week, and accuracy is about at the eighth week.

The requirement that a physician have two consultants and then present the case to the abortion committee is unsuited, and unsuited procedure for medical treatment.

Q   Yet, hasn't it been followed for years in accredited hospitals?

MRS. HAMES: There are many committees in hospitals; they have tissue committees, and they have other kinds of committees. But these do not make decisions about constitutional right, and whether or not it will be exercised. And the hospital abortion committee, being a statutory committee, is the arm of the State Government, we contend, and would be different from a mere tissue committee through which it is - -

Q   As I understood, you were arguing this as being unduly cumbersome; and my response is: It is not a fact that this has been a routine in accredited hospitals all over the country for many, many years?

MRS. HAMES: It is my understanding that the accreditation standards of the Joint Commission do not require appointment of abortion or other committees. This is a practice that has developed and grown up; and I think it grew up prior to the American Law Institute, specifically as to abortion. And it was to relieve doctors from their responsibility in making this decision solely. And they were afraid of assuming that responsibility because of the criminal sanctions imposed by law.

Therefore, they had their hospitals constitute abortion committees, who would help share the responsibility for such a decision.

The operation of committees of a hospital, of course, would be an internal matter for hospitals, and it might be possible that a committee - - that a hospital could continue to have a committee to govern abortions in that hospital.

However, it's our contention that the right to have — to terminate a pregnancy should not be controlled by a statutory committee from which there is no appeal, where there is no opportunity for a hearing; the woman is never seen by the members of the committee, she is never told why her abortion was denied, and her doctor, many times, is not even permitted to come and present her case.

This committee, we feel, is not a vehicle which could properly determine this constitutional right. We feel that it is, as the court said below, a medical-personal decision; that many factors in deciding whether to have an abortion are personal. Like your desire to have only two children, or your family size; your economic status is a matter of personal knowledge.

This is not a matter that can be effectively presented to a committee; a doctor could not possibly present all these matters to a hospital abortion committee. And we feel that this committee is just an improper vehicle for determining the right to terminate an unwanted pregnancy.

Additionally, there is the problem of the doctor, and he feels that his patient should have an abortion, she wants an abortion; but he must submit his decision not only to concurrence of two more consultants, but to the hospital abortion committee.

These are his competitors, his professional competitors;

they are doctors in his community who decide what he will do in his medical practice. It's the position of the doctors that this infringes their right to practice medicine in accordance with their best medical judgment. It permits the committee to substitute their judgment, their religious or personal views with those of his and the decision reached between himself and his patient.

Q   Well, that argument would be true about the maintenance of professional standards generally in the medical profession, would it not?   Disciplinary proceedings, and everything else.   Presumably those who pass upon malpractice or lack of professional competence or ethical judgement on the part of doctors are his competitors.

MRS. HAMES: That's true; but I would think that he has some voice in arriving at the standards of his profession, and that the application of his professional standards would not be the same as application of his - - of the abortion committee's on personal views.

I think that these are matters that are better left to the profession; I would think that the medical profession can develop its standards. The American College of Obstetricians and Gynecologists has taken the policy that where an abortion is requested by a woman, and there are no contra-medical indications, then the abortion will be performed without even the necessity of a consultant. Where it is recommended by a doctor, then the American College recommends that the doctor have a consultant on that decision.

I think that the profession can develop standards, and that this is where it should be controlled, rather then by a hospital abortion committee sitting in a quasi-judicial situation.

I would point out that the hospital accreditation requirement limits abortions in Georgia, and denies many rural woman of access to abortion services: 105 of Georgia's counties have no accredited hospitals, so that those women who are dependent upon their county hospital for pre-medical service are denied, by virtue of this hospital accreditation requirement, their - -

Q   How many of those counties have no hospitals at all?

MRS. HAMES: There are 284 hospitals, and I have not made a comparison to see. Abortions have only been performed in 22 counties in Georgia.

Q   Well, isn't it possible that some of these counties to which you refer do not have hospitals at all?

MRS. HAMES: Yes, it is possible, Your Honor, that some eight or ten of the smaller, less-populated hospitals — counties could have that situation.

Q   Well, if that's all there are in Georgia, with the larger number of counties you have, I think you have more counties than any other State, don't you?

MRS. HAMES: I believe we do.

Q   You're far better developed than many other States. I just question your general statement about denial of relief - -

MRS. HAMES: One further thing - -

Q   - - generally as to counties.

MRS. HAMES: Excuse me.

- - as to hospitals. The New York experience has shown

that abortions in clinics is a relatively safe — is a safe procedure. There the abortions, early abortions, are not required to
be performed in hospitals. And if we had this requirement or
did not have the limitation to accredited hospitals in Georgia,
then we could have abortion clinics in the more rural areas.

Q   This Georgia legislation is relatively recent, isn't it?
MRS. HAMES: It was adopted in 1968, April of 1968.

**Q   May I be clear as to the relief you're asking: You
got a declaratory judgment, declaring that some
provisions of the Georgia statute are unconstitutional?**
MRS. HAMES: That's correct.

**Q   And you're asking a declaratory judgment,
declaring the entire statute unconstitutional?**
MRS. HAMES: Yes, sir.

Q   And you want us to do that?
MRS. HAMES: Yes, Your Honor.

**Q   And then you want us to order and issue an in-
junction against all future enforcement statutes, is that
it?**

MRS. HAMES: That's correct. Or other application of the law, meaning, by abortion committees of hospitals.

Q And, as I understand it, you are arguing the constitutional rights of Mary Doe and the physicians here?

MRS. HAMES: That's correct.

Q Am I correct in not detecting any constitutional argument on behalf of your other plaintiffs, your registered nurses, your counselors and the rest?

MRS. HAMES: As to the nurses, we would say that they still have a controversy or a need for relief, because they, too, are not permitted to practice their profession. Of course they would not be independently performing abortions but would be assisting doctors. So that there is.

As to the ministers and other counselors, social workers who wish to counsel abortions, based - - under the decision below which said that abortions are obtainable for any reason, they would not now fear the prosecution under the conspiracy statutes or the aiding and abetting statutes for counseling abortions. There's no real relief needed here. We - -

Q Well, relief may be needed, but are you making a constitutional argument on behalf of the nurses, counselors, ministers, and what-have-you?

MRS. HAMES: On behalf of the nurses, yes, Your Honor. And as for the counselors, it is our contention that they had a sufficient collision of interests for the declaratory relief to be granted as to them.

Q As a - -

Q Well, do I detect that you're not making a constitutional argument with respect to them? If it's only a need for declaratory relief, isn't that a State law matter?

MRS. HAMES: We occupy a position similar to Texas, as to declaratory relief. We have a statute in Georgia which says that equity will not interfere in the administration of criminal laws, or of - - yes, criminal laws. This has recently been construed, in 1968, to prohibit a declaratory judgment in equitable relief as to a criminal statute.

So that there is no alternative to go into State court for declaratory relief.

And this is the only form in which we contend that plaintiffs could assert their rights.

Q   Well, I still don't know whether you're making a constitutional argument.

MRS. HAMES: Yes, we are making a constitutional argument for everyone in this - -

Q   With respect to all the plaintiffs?

MRS. HAMES: With respect to - - including the First Amendment argument which was made below as to counseling abortions.

Q   I didn't get that from your brief, but I'm glad to be straightened out.

MRS. HAMES: Thank you, Your Honor.

Q   Mrs. Hames, just before you sit down, perhaps you made this clear but it hasn't been made clear to me. You're appealing here because, while you want at least a partial victory by way of a declaratory judgment, you were denied an injunction and that is what, technically, is giving you a right to appeal directly to this Court: the denial of the injunction.

You're arguing now that you should have - - wholly have had a complete victory on the merits, that the entire statute should have been stricken. And also that an injunction should have issued.

And I'm asking you, in that connection, that second connection, whether the Georgia authorities had disregarded or manifested an intent to disregard the Federal District Court's declaratory judgment of the invalidity of the substantive part of this statute?

MRS. HAMES: No, Mr. Justice, there has been no manifestation on - -

Q You were here, I think, in the argument of the previous case - -

MRS. HAMES: Yes.

Q - - where that was true, apparently, in Texas?

MRS. HAMES: Yes.

I think the need for injunctive relief arises from the fact that out of the 24 appellate decisions on abortion in Georgia, 13 of those have involved doctors. So that there - - we have a history of prosecution of doctors in Georgia.

Additionally, the law is continued to be enforced, and abortions are being denied, for unknown reasons, by the hospital abortion committee. That presents a very real need for injunctive relief there.

Q Do I understand you correctly that no hospital abortion committee has said, We're denying this because we're not going to follow the District Court's judgment in this case?

MRS. HAMES: We don't know why they're denying the abortions. They are not required to disclose, and they do not disclose.

Q And you said of 24 appellate decisions, 13 involve doctors?

MRS. HAMES: Yes, Your Honor.

Q What did the other 13 involve?

MRS. HAMES: Contractors.

Q The other 11, I mean.

MRS. HAMES: Yes.

"Plumbers", abortionists.

Illegal abortionists.

Q   Non-physicians, you mean?

MRS. HAMES: Yes, non-physicians. Yes.

Q   I see. Thank you.

MRS. HAMES: Thank you.

MR. CHIEF JUSTICE BURGER: Mrs. Beasley.

ORAL ARGUMENT OF MRS. DOROTHY T. BEASLEY,

ON BEHALF OF THE APPELLEES

MRS. BEASLEY: Mr. Chief Justice, and may it please the Court:

The very nut of the argument before this Court and the issue facing this Court is the value which is to be placed on fetal life.

The State, in this case, takes the position that fetal life is to be protected, that it is a protectable interest.

Now, the question is whether there should be no value placed on it, so that a woman may, in her own decision and with her own doctor, determine, without any intervention by the State, that she may abort a pregnancy after she has conceived and is carrying a live, human fetus.

Or whether, on the other hand, the State itself may protect the interests of that fetus in any regard.

The court below determined that the State's interest - - the State was attempting to go too far in protecting fetal life; but that it could protect it to some degree because it could prohibit those abortions which were not necessary in the best clinical judgment of the physician, taking into consideration not only medical factors but really everything involved in the particular case: the woman's economic position; her family position and so on.

But, at any rate, the court did indicate that the State had an interest in protecting fetal life at least to that extent.

Now, if the court, of course, had said, Well you can have an abortion in any event, whether it's necessary or not, then, of course, it would be consistent with the argument that's made by the appellant.

However, they said the State does have an opportunity to control those abortions which are not necessary. They may prohibit them, period.

I think a great mistake has been made by that court, and

by appellants, in saying that the purpose of the statute is single; that is, that it is only a health measure.

In the first place, it's in the criminal code. As a separate bill, it was introduced to amend a part of the criminal code.

The original bill, or the original statute, in 1876, was a criminal action. And it speaks of the unborn child. It doesn't speak of a "thing" or an "organism", but it speaks of protecting the unborn child. And that is at least one of the interests of the State in this statute.

I submit that there are three. If you read the whole statue in its entirety. No. 1, and the underlying reason, is the protection of fetal life from wanton or arbitrary destruction simply upon the convenience or the desire of the woman who is bearing it.

Secondly, of course, the State is interested in protecting women who are going to undergo a very serious procedure at any stage, and that is the abortion procedure.

And that, of course, is indicated by the very serious procedure that's set out, by not only having her own physician think that she could have one, but is getting consultants and also approval by the hospital abortion committee, and requiring it to be done in a hospital. Which, by the way, has certainly been the position of the American Medical Association in the House of Delegates in 1967, which was just one year prior to the time this statute was enacted, and has, in my understanding at least, been the position of the American College of Obstetricians and Gynecologists in their standards.

And in their latest standard with regard to abortion, as I read it, and of course this is not before the Court, and I just make an aside for a moment to say that that's part of the trouble with this case: it's a facial attack on the constitutionality of the statute. And all of these statistics and what the doctors think on one side or on the other, and whether abortions are safer than childbirth, and so on, are really not before the Court because they were not introduced into evidence in the court below.

So they are not part of the record.

Now, certainly, the appellants tried to present evidence, and in the only hearing that was held before the lower court, which hearing lasted about two hours, at the most, there was only argument, but both sides came prepared to present evidence.

And of course in order to attack the constitutionality as to its effect or its operation in Georgia, or its applicability, I submit that we would need a fuller record; and that if there is an attack on the face of the statute, it cannot be supported without looking at these further facts, unless you can say that the State has no interest whatsoever in protecting fetal life.

And I think that the interest which the fetus has, as a human fetus, in this instance becomes broader as time goes on.

I think the State has a greater obligation to protect that fetal life today than it did in 1876. And for this reason: it's more protectable now than it ever was before.

There are more methods now that can be used to protect it, including blood transfusions and surgery while it's still in the womb.

Now, this, I think, has been brought to the Court's attention in some of the briefs that have been filed by the physicians. But, at any rate, there are more possible ways now - - for example, the very growth of the science of fetology, which is, of course, the treatment of the fetus before it's born.

So its development, it has been created, and its development up to the period of birth is such now that it can be protected by the State, and so I think there is a greater duty upon the State to do so.

Now, the question which I think comes here with regard to these exceptions is a balancing of competing interests. The State certainly takes no position that the woman has constitutional right to abortion.

We have not been shown where that right emanates from. If it emanates from the considerations which were given in the Griswold case, I think it's erroneous, because in that case there was not the introduction of another entity. A person has a right to be let alone, certainly; but not when another person is involved, or another human entity is involved.

The same thing with the marriage relationship. Here a third entity is involved, and the State says you may not indiscriminately dispose of or discontinue the life of that third entity except in special circumstances.

Now, this is where we get to the competing interest and

the balancing of the interest, which, by the way, I think was the statement in recognition that former Mr. Justice Clark made in his Law Review article about the State being in position to balance competing interest. That is, you have a fetus growing in a woman on one side, and the woman says she doesn't want it, you've got a clash of interests there.

Now, the State has taken the position: Well, we're not going to prohibit all abortions, because we understand that there are circumstances in which a woman should be able to destroy the fetus, because her interest in superior.

And there are three broad reasons now that are given in our statute, of course, which were struck out by the court below, so that we can't here really argue those, although we attempted to bring an appeal here, which was denied for lack of jurisdiction; and our appeal now is awaiting its further pursuit in the Fifth Circuit.

Q Well, Mrs. Beasley, I don't see why you can't argue that here. Your position is that the court was right in no issuing an injunction, and you can support that position

by any argument you want. You're the appellee, you're not the appellant.

MRS. BEASLEY: Thank you very much.

{Laughter.]

Underlying the exceptions, the reason for the exceptions in the statute, is the broad principle of self-preservation. We recognize that a human being has the right ultimately of self-defense. And I think that these exceptions are manifestations of that.

We allow a woman to abort a fetus if it is the product of rape. Now, that a has been construed in our State to also include incest.

This is the product, of course, in that situation, of an unwarranted, uninvited attack on her. And to require her to bear that child is almost a punishment; or at least she would often regard it as a punishment. So here she can defend herself from that fetus by destroying it.

Secondly, as far as a fetus which is gravely malformed and will be permanently malformed, or deficient, the State recognizes, I think, a very practical exception because it recognizes that in most cases she is the one who is going to have to raise that child; and the State is not now in the position where it can automatically take in all of these children. And of course it would be a great deal of heartbreak to her; and so it would involve her own well-being. And the State says, in these circumstances science is not enough developed so that we can correct these deformities, the State can't help enough in these circumstances, and therefore we regard it as an exception an allow you to defend yourself against the circumstance which would arise if you had to bear and keep this child.

The third one, of course, is the preservation of her own life or her own health; and of course it has been construed — not judicially but as a matter of practice — that health here includes mental health.

Now, - -

Q   Did you say that the first one you mentioned, which is the third one, I think, in the statute — pregnancy resulting from forcible or statutory rape — also includes — by construction also includes pregnancy resulting from incest?

MRS. BEASLEY: Yes, I did. And I say this only from an observation of the reports that have been collected by the Georgia Department of Public Health, to whom all abortions, of course, are reported.

That, again, is not in the record because there was no evidence presented. However, particularly since the period of the court decision, the reasons that are reported in by the physicians that are performing abortions have been expanded, so that no only have you got rape and incest as separate, and not only do you have for mental problems or physical problems that are maternal, you also have economic and social now being given as a separate category and reason.

So that places it at a point that an injunction is not needed, also.

Q   Yes, but, incidentally, I gather no court below said that that's the correct interpretation of this point?

MRS. BEASLEY: That's right. But no one has brought the matter to the attention of the Georgia courts. And I would dispute - -

Q Well, you say this has happened since this court decision, though; didn't you?

That's the - - so it's the effect of the decision, is it not?

MRS. BEASLEY: As far as the social and economic - -

Q Yes.

MRS. BEASLEY: - - is concerned, I think your question as to the rape or incest is what existed before. I'm not certain of that, but I think it would, because the court decision would make no distinction or voiding it, necessarily, in that regard.

Q Well, the statute does not mention incest.

MRS. BEASLEY: That is correct. But I - -

Q And it clearly does not mention economic or social conditions - -

MRS. BEASLEY: Clearly.

Q - - and now, if abortions are taking place, based upon those extra-statutory reasons, I would suppose that this has begun to happen since this case was decided by the District Court. Is that true?

MRS. BEASLEY: Yes, indeed, it has happened since then,

and I think that's one of the very reasons why no injunction would be necessary.

In the first place, the parties against whom the - -

Q Well, is that the State thrust, to the extent the judgment below was affirmed, Georgia accepts it and would not prosecute under the statute - -

MRS. BEASLEY: Until it's changed, otherwise. But the State, of course, takes the position that the statute is constitutional as it was written.

Q Yes, I know, but my prophesy was if the judgment below were to be affirmed.

MRS. BEASLEY: If the judgment below were to be affirmed, certainly there is no indication that the State and the District Attorneys and the hospital abortion committees would not follow the mandate of this Court, as has been done; no prosecutions have been brought, despite the fact of the reporting of these other extra-statutory abortions.

Q Relying on the judgment below -- you reportedly rely on the judgment below, in these positions, I gather - -

MRS. BEASLEY: That is correct.

Q - - in performing abortions, relying on the judgment as permitting abortions?

MRS. BEASLEY: Yes, indeed.

And so there would be no purpose for an injunction because it's being obeyed as a declaratory judgment.

Moreover, an injunction against any one of the defendant parties would really lead nowhere, because the Attorney General, of course, is not one to bring prosecutions in the first place, and has no connections whatsoever with these hospital abortion committees, despite what the court below believed.

Another suit, as a matter of fact, was instituted last year against the Fulton-DeKalb Hospital Authority, a body politic and corporate, doing business as Grady Memorial Hospital.

Now, that's where you get the abortion committee in the hospital. And the Attorney General has no idea what the abortion committee in this particular cases did, or how much it knew. And that again is one of the great problems with this case.

We know of no facts, there are no facts in this case, no established facts.

Q   Why was it the three-judge court did not permit the introduction of evidence?

MRS. BEASLEY: The court apparently believed that it was not necessary, because they were going to consider it as a facial attack only.   And I think the court made a mistake in that circumstance.   I think they confused these two things: one, whether you need facts to establish a justiciable controversy and, two, whether you need facts and a concrete circumstance in order to decide facial unconstitutionality.

And I think they jumped to the second situation, and said, Well, we're going to just look at that statute anyway, so the facts don't matter.

And I would submit that that's a wrong circumstance, even the - -

Q   Are you - - do you say there was or wasn't a case or controversy?

MRS. BEASLEY: I say there was not. There was not a case or controversy.

The Attorney General, the District Attorney of Fulton

County, and the chief of police of the City of Atlanta had no case or controversy whatsoever with Mary Doe or any of the doctors or organizations or ministers or counselors.

Q   Well, say a person alleges that she is pregnant and has tried to get an abortion and been refused.

MRS. BEASLEY: I think the controversy is with the - - whoever denied the abortion. That is, it may have been the committee. I think that that would have to - - they would have to be an important party.

Q   Let's assume, though, that there is - - that their refusal to abort is wholly consistent with the law, and that the refusal was precisely what the law required them to do. Then who is the controversy with?

MRS. BEASLEY: I think you would indeed have a case or controversy there.

Q   With the Attorney General?

MRS. BEASLEY: No, sir, not with the Attorney General; with those who are implementing the law. The Attorney General would be interested and would undoubtedly - - as required by law, he would file a brief.

Q   If a doctor refuses an abortion because he's afraid of criminal prosecution, I suppose one effective way to resolve the controversy is to enjoin the person who might prosecute.

MRS. BEASLEY: And that's not the Attorney General.

Q   Who is it?

MRS. BEASLEY: IT would be the District Attorney.

Q   He's one of the appellees here?

MRS. BEASLEY: Yes, he is one of the appellees, Mr. Justice Douglas.

Q   So is the chief of police.

MRS. BEASLEY: that is indeed correct. Of course the chief of police would not bring the prosecution, and there was no prosecutions or threats - -

Q   Well, I know, but isn't there a case or controversy - - if a woman had been refused an abortion, and because a doctor is afraid of being prosecuted, don't you have a controversy with the law enforcement officers who are enforcing the law?

MRS. BEASLEY: Yes, you may; but there was no enforcement here which was threatened or impending.

Q   Well, but it was conduct pursuant to the law, though, mainly in the refusal of an abortion - -

MRS. BEASLEY: But we don't know that it was pursuant to the law. You're assuming, I belief, another circumstance: that there was compliance with the law. That's what the State - -

Q   What did the complaint allege?

MRS. BEASLEY: It alleged that that was the reason, but again, they also stated that they didn't know.

Q   When do you decide standing, after a trial or on the face of a complaint?

MRS. BEASLEY: I'm sorry; I didn't hear your question.

Q   When do you decide standing, after a trial?

MRS. BEASLEY: No, sir; I think that it must appear in the - as the case proceeds.

Q   All right, well, let's assume the facts are true as alleged in the complaint.   Case or controversy?

MRS. BEASLEY: I think there aren't enough facts there. No. No case or controversy. Not with these defendants.

MR. CHIEF JUSTICE BURGER: We will continue after lunch.

MRS. BEASLEY: Thank you.

(Whereupon, at 12:00 noon, the Court was recessed, to reconvene at 1:00 p.m., the same day.)

AFTERNOON SESSION

MR. CHIEF JUSTICE BURGER: You may proceed, Mrs. Beasley.

MRS. BEASLEY: Thank you, Mr. Chief Justice.

We were speaking, I think, when we stopped about case or controversy. And I think that it's very clear that a case or controversy would exist with a hospital or hospital abortion committee in all of the constitutional questions which are sought to be raised and argued in this case put before it there.

I think also, that - -

Q   I suppose if your requirement was satisfied, and they would show the threat, you would then conclude it would be beyond the competence of the three-judge court to enter a decree?

MRS. BEASLEY: That's correct. If there were that. But here we have no case or controversy, and the threat of course would involve the anti-injunction statute, I think rather then whether it could be - -

Q   Well, a threat would make it a case or controversy.

MRS. BEASLEY: A threat might.

Q   Yes.

MRS. BEASLEY: If the proper parties were involved. But here, for example, we don't have - - as far as we know, we don't have Mary Doe's doctor, someone who is taking any action; and even in the cases which the Court recently has considered, about the facial constitutionality of some criminal statutes, there was an actual case or controversy - - not even with regard to the – -

Q   Well, Mary Doe's real, isn't she?

MRS. BEASLEY: I don't know.

Q   I thought it was conceded that she was.

MRS. BEASLEY: No, sir. We know no facts about her at all. We assume that since there is an affidavit concerning it, that those facts may very well be true; but we have had no opportunity to see whether there other facts.

Q Did the - - as I remember, your colleague on the other side answered that there was an offer of proof to the District Court, that she was real, and that he said that wasn't necessary.

MRS. BEASLEY: That is correct.

Q That means he accepted. Did he accept the fact that this was a real human being, a person?

MRS. BEASLEY: The court below accepted, as far as I know, the statements that were made in allegation as being true. So that no proof was submitted, no interrogatories were answered; we had no opportunity to find out.

Q But it was - - but the plaintiff expressed a willingness and did offer to show this; is that correct?

MRS. BEASLEY: Yes, through counsel.

Q Yes.

MRS. BEASLEY: That is correct.

Q I understand she was in the courtroom.

MRS. BEASLEY: That is what counsel informs us is correct, but she was not pointed out, she didn't stand up in court, for example, and indicate herself to the court. But we just understand that she was there. We don't know who she was, there was a courtroom full of people.

So that we couldn't follow up, you see, in any way.

Q   Yes

Q   Once it's accepted, what difference does it make to the case, if any?

MRS. BEASLEY: Pardon? I'm sorry.

Q   Once that's accepted as a fact, why will that make any difference to the case?

MRS. BEASLEY: If her allegations are accepted?

Q   If the proffer, if the court says the proffer of proof was unnecessary, then why do we need be concerned about whether she is a fictitious or a real person?

MRS. BEASLEY: Because it was not a complete divulgence of the facts surrounding circumstance. For example, we don't know that the hospital abortion committee knew as much about her as in her allegation. We don't know the real person for which they denied her the abortion. Particularly since she was, assertedly, granted the approval of another hospital abortion committee; which, again, makes her situation somewhat moot. Because she did receive - -

Q   If you should lose on your point that there's no case or controversy, do you concede that the remedy given was proper?

MRS. BEASLEY: No, sir. Mr. Justice Douglas, we think that the statute itself, in toto, does not render any lack of due process or equal protection on its facts, to any of these plaintiffs or anyone else. We think that the statute is a constitutional one as written.

Q   Suppose you lose on that, do you think the remedy as given was improper?

MRS. BEASLEY: If this Court decides that the restrictions that were made on the statute are correct, and a declaratory judgment should issue, we would think that would indeed be proper; and that in injunction would not be necessary.

Q   Do you think an injunction would be proper in light of 1983?

MRS. BEASLEY: We think not, because we find no necessity, and of course an injunction is an extraordinary legal relief. Injunction against any one of these appellees would do nothing, as far as the enforcement, that isn't already being done, as far as the statue is concerned.

Q   But you would construe the word "inequity" in 1983 as allowing an injunction? In some cases?

MRS. BEASLEY: There may be a situation in which an injunction would be inappropriate, but not in this circumstance, where there is no - - well, if the Court considers that there is a case or controversy, there still would not be a need for an injunction; of course, an injunction being a discretionary type of thing. And the court below finding no necessity for one, we thing that was a correct finding by the court. And so there should be no necessity for this Court to direct - -

Q   So a declaratory decree would be proper under 1983?

MRS. BEASLEY: Yes sir.

Q   And then, of course, I suppose the Court could, in the interest of effectuating its declaratory judgment, at some later time issue an injunction; couldn't it?

MRS. BEASLEY: Yes, sir. If it became necessary.

Q   That would be if there were indications that the declaratory judgment were not being otherwise obeyed or effectuated.

MRS. BEASLEY: Yes, indeed. I think that there would be a continuing opportunity to do so.

Q   Fine. We don't have here, Mrs. Beasley, do we, any question of the application of 2283? There was no pending State - -

MRS. BEASLEY: No, sir.

Q   - - proceeding of any kind, was there?

MRS. BEASLEY: No.

Q   Civil or criminal?

MRS. BEASLEY: No, Mr. Justice Stewart, there were no - - nothing at all, as far as that's concerned, not even a threat. And I think that's one of the things that makes it so different from the <u>Wisconsin vs. Constantineau</u> case, where there was something actually done; it was conduct there.

Q   Right.

MRS. BEASLEY: Taken on behalf of the officials of the State, in that case the chief of police, I believe it was.

Q   Right.

MRS. BEASLEY: Which we don't have here at all.

I would like to point out one other thing, though, we were - - I was mentioning to the Court the purposes of the statute. I think one of the other purposes of it - - I think there are primarily three - - being to protect fetal life and of course the health of the mother, in having to go through this procedure, and also to protect doctors who are going to perform therapeutic abortions. The procedure is set out and they're protected if they stay within those wide protections that are given in the statute, the procedure that's given, the District Attorney has no basis on which to prefer an indictment against them; and of course the burden would be on him to show that the abortion was not necessary.

So I think the statute is also to protect the doctors so that they can operate with regard to therapeutic abortions.

Q   Well, isn't the doctor already protected — you don't have any criminal prosecution for any other operation, do you?

MRS. BEASLEY: That's correct.

Q   In Georgia?

You don't, do you?

MRS. BEASLEY: No, it does not; not that I know of.

Q   Then why do they need that protection on abortions?

MRS. BEASLEY: Because abortions - -

Q   Because the abortion statute is there.

MRS. BEASLEY: That's right.

Q   That's what I thought.

MRS. BEASLEY: One other point I would like to make, and that is this: In another area the State does recognize fetal life as being human life, and that is with regard to fetal death certificates, which are required to be filed when there is a fetal death.

In that portion of the statute which deals with funeral arrangements and so on, vital records, the distinction is made between live birth and fetal death. Live birth is regarded as a situation where a product of conception, at whatever stage it occurs, is expelled or extracted from a mother's womb, and there is evidence of life: which means — and some examples are giben in the statute — voluntary muscle movement or heartbeat, or something that indicates breathing or movement, some independent activity in that fetal life. And that's regarded as a live birth.

A fetal death is regarded as that type of extraction where there is no evidence of life.

So I think in that instance, too, the State carries forward the consistent concept and attitude towards pre-birth children, in that they are indeed human life that needs to be recorded, and that should be very carefully watched before there is any destruction of it.

It think that; in closing, I would like to just say that we look at a criminal defendant and say, before he is going to be condemned, his guilt must be proved beyond a reasonable doubt. Now, we look at an unborn child and say, Can we not at least limit the destruction of his life to these certain circumstances, or is he, as an innocent human life, allowed to be extinguished without any regard whatsoever?

Thank you.

MR. CHIEF JUSTICE BURGER: Thank you, Mrs. Beasley.